Y0-AHQ-471

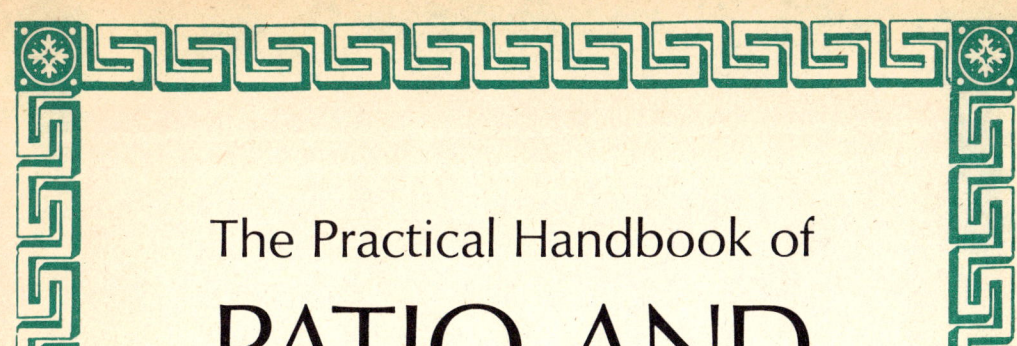

The Practical Handbook of
PATIO AND OUTDOOR PROJECTS

By Tom Philbin

Fawcett Publications, Inc.
1515 Broadway
New York, New York 10036

FRANK BOWERS: *Editor-in-Chief*

WILLIAM MIUCCIO: *Art Editor* • MICHAEL GAYNOR: *Asst. Art Editor*

ARNOLD E. SYLVESTER: *Marketing Director*

ELLEN MEYER: *Editor*

Editorial Staff: DAN BLUE, ELLENE SAUNDERS, JOE CORONA, CAROL FRIEDMAN, COLLEEN KATZ, MARION LYONS

Art Staff: JACK LA CERRA, ED WERTH, CARRIE SCHLIEPER, WENDY STONE

LAUREL KURNIDES: *Production Manager*

How-To Art by Eugene Thompson
Cover Color by Filon, Sakrete and Coleco
All photos not credited are by the author

No part of this book may be reproduced in any form without permission in writing from the publisher, except by a reviewer who wishes to quote brief passages in connection with a review written for inclusion in a magazine, newspaper or broadcast.

Printed in U.S.A. by
FAWCETT PRINTING CORPORATION
Rockville, Maryland

Copyright © MCMLXXV by Fawcett Publications, Inc.
All Rights Reserved

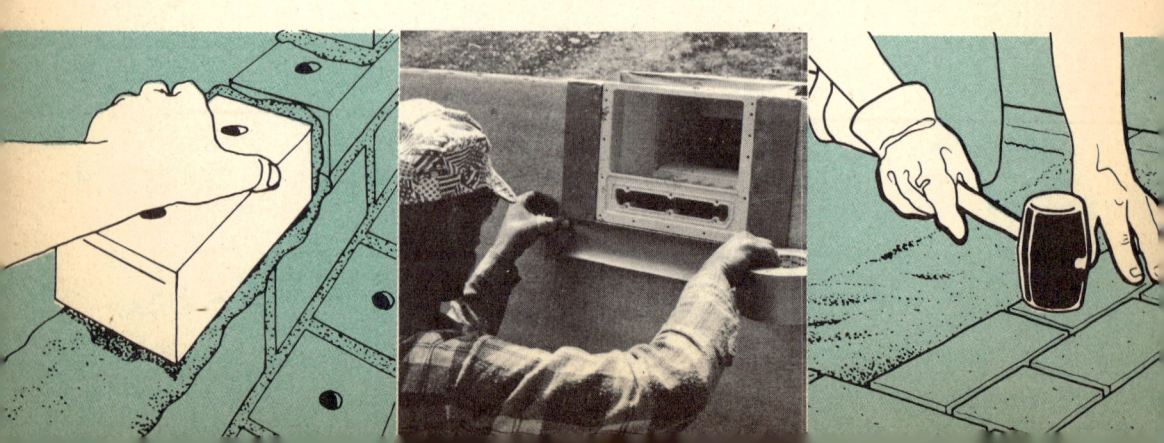

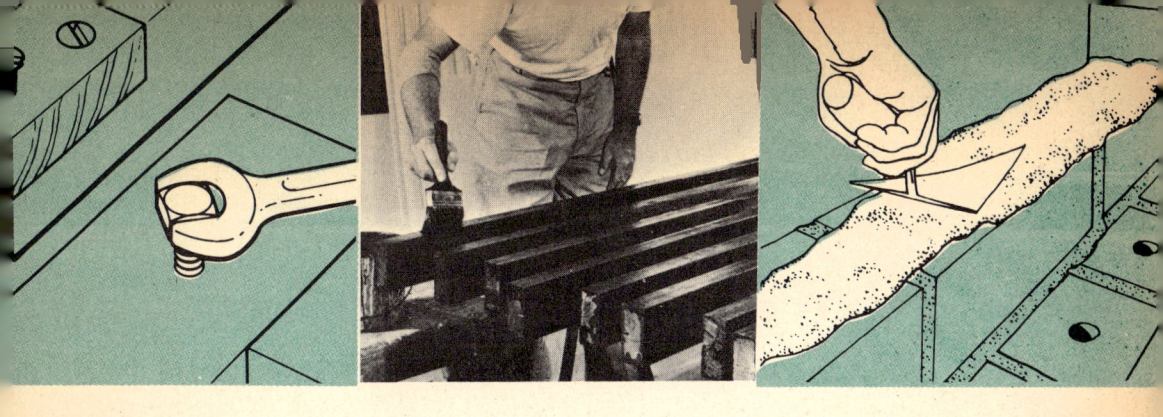

CONTENTS

A Primer On Patios	5
Installing A Patio Door	10
Building Patios	16
Dressing Up A Drab Slab	23
Decks To Delight	28
Let (Not) The Sunshine In	36
Outdoor Furniture	43
Barbecues You Can Build	50
Miscellaneous Projects	58
Outdoor Storage	68
Fencing Facts	78
A Cool Way To Beat The Heat	87
A Place For Your Car	94
ABC's Of Steps	104
A New Driveway	110
Outdoor Lighting	116
Budget Landscaping	123

INTRODUCTION

In recent years the concept of outdoor living has been adopted by more and more families. Basically, all it means is that the family gets as much enjoyment from activities conducted outside as inside.

To do this, the outdoor living environment—the patio and its environs—must be properly equipped; stocked, as it were, with all the things an individual family needs to get the maximum enjoyment with the least inconvenience.

The thrust of this book is concerned with helping you, the handyman, equip it yourself. I've striven to include plans and ideas for the things anyone would need.

Most basic, of course, is the patio itself —your outdoor floor. I've included a variety of these so that you can select what's right in terms of your outdoor decor, your budget, the size you need, your handyman skills and other considerations.

Indeed, selection is a "theme" I've tried to incorporate in all the chapters. There are *different* storage units, *different* ways to dress up a drab slab, *different* ways to build decks and patio covers, a wealth of *different* fencing ideas, *different* pools, *different* fun ideas for kids, a host of *different* lighting possibilities. (The latter area, by the way, is really something to explore. Given the proper illumination, there's no reason at all why outdoor living cannot be enjoyed at night as well as when the sun is shining.)

If the driving theme of the book is to enable you to make your outdoor living area an outdoor living room, I have included other projects as well, because homeowners have a crying need for more information on them. For example, there are instructions on how to build a driveway. Not just any driveway, but one that will last for years without cracking. Elsewhere, you'll find information on making simple edgings and retaining walls, and information on how to make a variety of carports. This may not specifically relate to outdoor living, but it's an essential consideration if you find yourself needing more space: You can convert the garage to a room and yet not make an orphan of your car.

All in all, I hope you find the book useful, and that you not only *build* many useful projects, but *enjoy* doing them. I'm sure you will.

Tom Philbin

A PRIMER ON PATIOS

Key to outdoor living is the patio. Here are the kinds you can build.

Stage center for outdoor living is the patio. Brick is just one of many types you can build.

The patio is stage center when it comes to outdoor living. Before you put one in, it will pay—literally and figuratively—to sit down and think and talk about it, carefully plan it with various considerations in mind. If you don't, there's always the danger of coming up with an ill-designed patio, which will be about as useful as a finished basement that's always damp.

ACCESSIBILITY

One thing to consider is its accessibility from the house. It should be easy to get to. If it isn't, it simply will not be used. Also, traffic that is routed through a room to get to wherever the patio will be should not disrupt the activities of anyone in that room. If, for example, you locate the patio right outside the kitchen (as most people do), you should have a separate entrance to it. Otherwise the homemaker will be disturbed in her activities.

SUN AND SHADE

Another thing to consider is sun—and shade. If you're the type who likes lots of sun, then it's probably wise to locate the patio where it will be in sun most of the day. If you don't like sun, though, you may not find it a comfortable, inviting place to go. Perhaps you can locate it so that a part of it is under shade most of the day. You and your wife can reserve that area and let the children, who usually don't mind weather as much as adults, have the sunny area.

Flagstone is one of the most beautiful, durable—and expensive—patio materials you can use. Careful placement of the pieces is required to avoid "crazy quilt" appearance.

On the other hand, if you must have constant shade, and you don't have the shade available, you'll have to build one of the shademakers described in Chapter 6. It should be part of your planning.

SIZE

How big should the patio be? If you have a lot of barbecues, entertain frequently, a large patio is usually called for. If not, a smaller one is usually adequate.

PRIVACY

How about privacy? It's usually a good idea, for you and your neighbors, to make the patio an "outdoor room" enclosed by fencing or shrubbery of some sort. But do consult with your neighbor before putting it in, not only to insure that the fencing is on your property, but just to be neighborly.

WIND

Wind is another consideration. This, of course, will vary according to where you live. In some areas you'll get a steady breeze, in others you won't. But the question is: Do you want that wind or not? In some areas it can be just as annoying as not having any breeze. Best bet is to check the area out before you put the patio in.

SHAPE

The shape the patio takes is yet another consideration. You needn't necessarily think in terms of the standard square or rectangular shape. How about an L-shape to utilize available space and get part of the patio under a shade tree? How about a round shape for the sheer good looks of it? It's your patio, and you needn't follow some mythical shape standards.

MATERIAL

The material you choose for the patio should harmonize with your house. You wouldn't want to use weathered brick, for example, if your house is ultra-modern looking.

Finally, there is the question of the material you should use to build the patio. Following is a roundup of what's available to help you decide what's best for you.

BRICK

Standard size of a brick is 8-inches long, 4-inches wide and 2¼-inches thick. You may think of it as just available in a reddish color. Actually, it's available in many different colors (black, white, tan, for example), in hundreds of shades and textures and glazed and unglazed.

In general, brick is a good material for the do-it-yourselfer. It comes in small units, making it easy to handle. It's durable. And, it's relatively inexpensive.

On the minus side, brick is very porous. If you spill some hot barbecue sauce on it, it will not be an easy task getting it up.

The longest lasting type of brick is "well burned," a deep red color, as opposed to the less durable so-called "green" type which is pinkish. Whatever kind of brick you buy, it's best to get it from one dealer all at once. Brick can vary slightly in color from batch to batch, and this can be noticeable on a patio.

FLAGSTONE

This is a truly beautiful outdoor flooring material, cut from natural colored rocks. Soft yellows, browns, greys, green and red are among the colors available. It can be laid with relative ease by the do-it-yourselfer directly on soil or a sand base, or in cement. It is also the most durable patio material you can buy.

Flagstone is available in thicknesses from ½ to 2-inches, either free form, natural shape or in rectangles. The big drawback of flagstone is price: It costs a minimum of four or five times as much as brick.

CONCRETE

This is such a familiar material that its virtues are perhaps not appreciated as well as some other materials. For one thing, it's durable. Also, it can be troweled or worked to a variety of textures, and by leaving the aggregate (stones or gravel that help give it strength) partially exposed, a distinctive look can be achieved. For another, it's not expensive.

On the minus side, concrete work can be backbreaking and, if you're not careful to install it properly (proper mix, grading, etc.) it can crack easily, something that often happens, even to pros.

You do not need to think of concrete as colorless. There are a number of ways to give it almost any coloration you wish (see Chapter 4).

If you live in a cold climate, consider using air-entrained concrete. This contains microscopic air bubbles that help solve the problem of cracking caused by freeze-thaw cycles. This type of concrete is also easier to work.

Plain old garden variety concrete takes on an elegant look when poured "in the round."

TILE

This is a thin, hard material with a sheen or glazed finish. It is available in a variety of sizes, ranging from 4x4-inches up to 12x12. Available in a variety of colors, you might think of tile as a particularly elegant material. It would go just as well inside the house as out (some people in mild climates use it to partially pave the entry way to a living room that is adjacent to a patio, continuing the tiles on the patio).

It can be installed on concrete, sand, or wood base, and has one excellent advantage: it's easy to clean. That barbecue sauce mentioned earlier would come up easily.

Tile has a number of disadvantages. It is expensive (double the cost of brick) and is difficult to cut. When wet it doesn't provide much traction. Most people favor tile as an accent material.

BLACKTOP (ASPHALT)

The big advantage of this material is that it's cheap. Not much (1½-inches) is all that is needed to provide a solid patio.

On the other hand, blacktop *is* black; as such, it retains and gives off tremendous heat, something that is not usually desirable on a patio. Also, it does soften and can be tracked around by shoes. And, it must be carefully installed and compacted to last—on a big area, it's definitely not a do-it-yourself job.

Most people favor blacktop as a topping for small paths and the like.

WOOD ROUNDS, BLOCKS, ETC.

Railroad ties, log "slices" and blocks can all be used for patio paving. Many people consider these quite handsome, a most natural and satisfying paving material. Also, wood in these forms is not expensive; many times you can pick up railroad ties, for example, from the local railroad yard if you're just willing to haul them away. And rounds, or blocks, can be chain-sawed

Patio blocks are easy to lay in a sand base. You may purchase them colored, or make your own with simple forms. Full instructions on how to do this are detailed later in text.

Portland Cement Assn.

Concrete "rounds" are simple to make. Colored stones are embedded in wet concrete. When partly dry, the concrete is brushed to expose stones. Rounds here are laid in gravel.

from any trees available.

These patio materials are not as long-lasting as stone or brick. They are subject to various degrees of stress from weather and insects. If you do opt for them, make sure that they have been soaked in a preservative that has been found best for your area (check at your lumberyard).

LOOSE FILL

There are a variety of materials that are known as loose fill: gravel, marble chips, wood chips, crushed brick, tanbark and the like.

These kinds of materials are usually used in conjunction with some other material, say concrete or flags, as accent materials. You may have a patio of concrete and then islands or paths between, filled with gravel or wood chips.

As a material for forming the entire patio floor, they're really not practical. They're difficult to walk on and pieces can be kicked all over the place (and gravel and power lawnmowers don't mix).

The big advantage of loose fills is low cost. You can cover a lot of area with them cheaply. In a pinch—financial—you could get by with a gravel patio. It's simple to install. Just spread it out directly on a leveled soil base, tamp (pack) it down, then water it so it settles some more and re-tamp. To retain it, however, you must first build some sort of concrete, wood or brick edging.

Sliding glass door gives easy access to outdoor living area, a must to insure area is used. *Andersen Windows*

INSTALLING A PATIO DOOR

Access to a patio is easy with sliding glass door. Build it simply.

No matter how livable you make your outdoor living area, it simply won't get used unless it's easily accessible from the inside of the house. A good way to insure this is to install a sliding glass door.

A sliding glass door works in two ways to make sure the area gets the use it should.

For one thing, it advertises that the area is there to be enjoyed. The large glass panels that comprise it let everyone see the area, unlike a regular solid door.

For another, you install it in the right location, perhaps in a family room with an outside wall facing the patio. It is natural, when the weather is nice, for traffic to flow between the two areas. In a sense, the patio becomes an extension of the family room.

DIFFERENT STYLES

Like windows, patio doors are available in various styles to harmonize with both interior and exterior decor. There is the

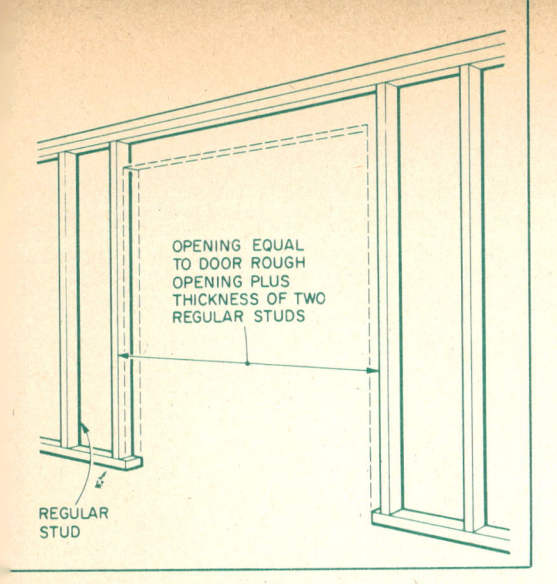

In frame construction, opening made in wall for door should be its width plus about 3".

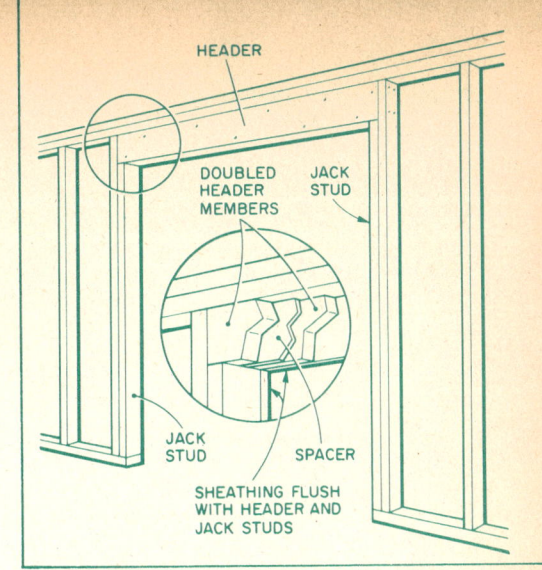

Key element in framing for door is size of header, which supports wall. Check text.

classic kind—two all-glass panels—but there are also glass-segmented units available to go with Colonial, French Provincial, Italian Provincial and other styles. For easier glass cleaning, many doors can be had with removable grill inserts. These snap on and off. When you have to clean the glass just snap the insert off. You clean one large expanse of glass instead of many small "windows" (or "lights," as they say in the trade).

Doors with some sort of decorative grillwork can be helpful from a safety point of view. While door glass on quality windows is thick, and tempered, it is also clear and hard-charging children have been known to bang into it.

Most commonly, doors are available with two panels, one fixed and the other sliding, with the sliding one either on the left or right side (as you look from outside) of the unit. You can also get units with three panels, (these are extra-wide, up to 12-feet), two fixed and one sliding in the middle.

You can get wood or aluminum doors. Aluminum is available in various finishes, including plain, white and bronze. Wood

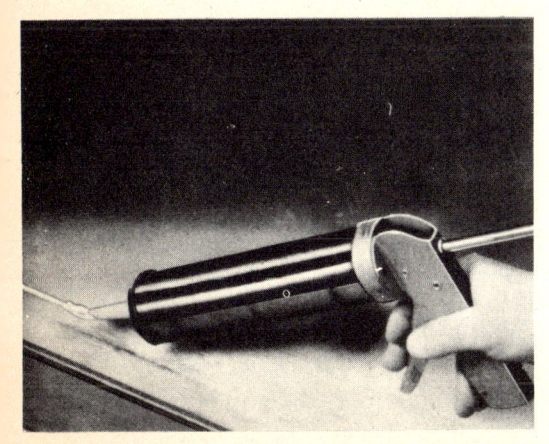

Before setting frame in place in open, run a bead of soft sealant where it will rest.

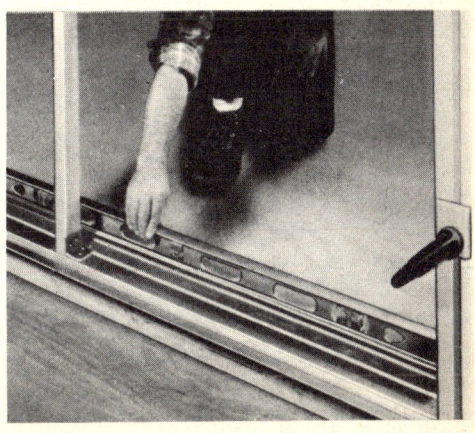

Check sill of frame for level when in place. You can hold it securely with C clamps.

11

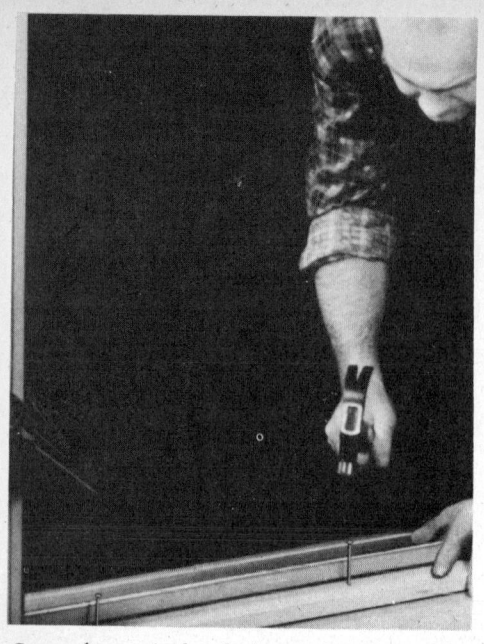

Once frame is level, fasten in place with some coated nails spaced a foot or so apart.

Use level to check trueness of frame. If frame isn't true, door won't open right.

Use cedar shingles wedges to get frame true. Shingles are tapered, ideal for the job.

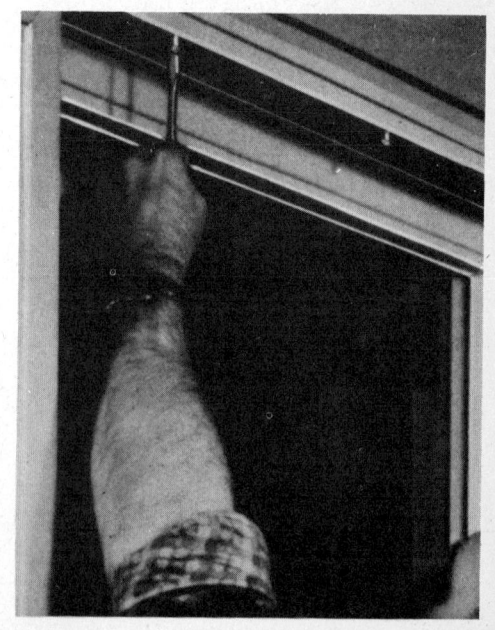

When true, screw jambs to trimmer (jack studs) and header (shown) with #10 screws.

Final step in installing frame is to nail on sill support using 8d nails, a foot apart.

Door consists of sliding and fixed section. Install fixed section, and brace it in place.

After securing fixed door, slip sliding door into track, carefully tipping it in at the top.

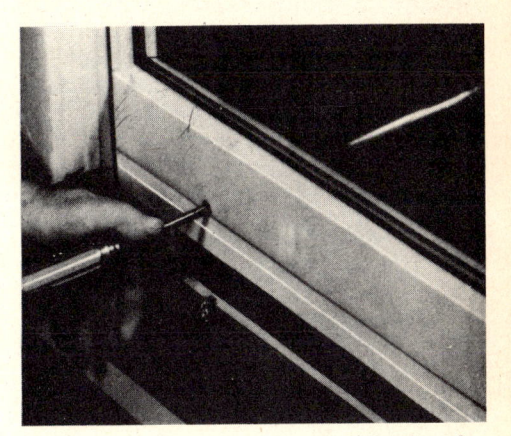

Final step is to adjust door so that it rides well. Adjusting sockets are on bottom rail.

doors come factory primed ready for painting or with parts covered in a rigid white vinyl sheathing that never requires painting.

Glass in the panel may simply be tempered or tempered and insulated—a sandwich of glass with a dead air space between. The insulating glass is a highly desirable feature and will pay for itself ultimately in fuel-cost savings.

Doors also come with rolling screen panels, handy on warm summer nights. You can let breezes in but keep insects out.

Depending on the manufacturer, doors come with the frame either knocked down or assembled. Panels always come pre-assembled.

LOCATION

First step in installing a patio door is to decide the best place to put it. Good locations are usually the family room, living room or basement, if that's converted into living area. Some people also locate it in a master bedroom wall.

For an easier installation, you can install it where there is a window or windows. Part of the opening you need in the wall is already there. In this situation, it is often the case that there is a radiator below the window. This, of course, must be moved, but it is not the big job it might seem to be. Unless you know how to do it, though, a professional should handle this aspect of the job.

OPENING UP THE WALL

Instructions will vary slightly from brand to brand of sliding glass door. Here, we show how to install an Andersen Perma-Shield Gliding Door. This is sheathed in semi-rigid white vinyl and doesn't need painting. It has double insulated tempered glass and is pre-weatherstripped. Wood is ponderosa pine.

In any case, the first step is to support the ceiling near where you're going to open up the wall. Four or five 2x4's, wedged in place between floor and ceiling will do it.

Working from the inside of the house, use a keyhole saw to carefully remove plasterboard from the inside, saw off unneeded bottom portions of studs. Remove siding and saw away sheathing. Now frame out the rough opening. Exactly how you frame will depend on whether the house is frame, brick or block construction. It also depends on the size of the door you're installing. Some typical situations are shown in the art. The key consideration, beyond the minor details of framing out, are the trimmer studs on the sides of the opening and the header that rests on them. These support everything above and must be beefy enough to do the job. Generally, 2x4 trimmer studs are fine, and a double 2x8 is good as a header for spans up to 12-feet. But do check with your local building code to be absolutely sure.

Another major concern is that the framework is true and level. If it isn't, you can run into problems getting the door true and level.

INSTALLING THE FRAME

First install the frame, then put in the door panel.

Use a block of wood to hammer in a vinyl flange in grooves around the top and

Patio door need not be one clear expanse of glass. Many-paned types are also available.

Bonus of any patio door is that it lets in a good deal of light, makes room seem larger.

sides of the door. Run a bead of soft sealing compound along the floor where the frame will sit, then position frame in opening from the outside, pushing it down to seat it firmly in the compound.

Check the sill for level. You can use C clamps to hold the frame securely in place.

After leveling, secure frame to floor with 8d coated nails along inside edge, spaced every foot or so.

Check sides, or jambs of frame, for true line. Use cedar shingles or thin wood wedges to shim out jambs to make true, holding jambs in position with C clamps.

Screw jambs to opening, driving No. 10, 2½-inch screws through pre-drilled holes. For an easier job, drill pilot holes in trimmer studs before driving screws.

Hold head part of frame in position. Make sure it is level. Then secure to header, driving No. 10 screws into pre-drilled holes.

Finally, place special sill support under protruding metal sill facing and secure with 8d box nails, 12-inches apart.

INSTALLING DOOR

The fixed section of the door goes in first. Position it in the outer run, or track, making sure it is true. Using blocks of wood, force door into side jamb track. When it is in tight, solid and true, secure it at top and bottom with sill brackets provided using No. 8, 1-inch screws. There are pre-drilled holes in the sill, head of frame and fixed panel, so getting these brackets in the proper position shouldn't be difficult.

Next, install with No. 8, 1½-inch screws (these have white heads) through parting stop into top rail of fixed door.

Now you're ready to install the moving door. Place it in opening on the inside track (it has rollers that slip into track). Then tip it in at the top.

Position the head stop piece—the piece that holds it in place—and secure piece with No. 7, 1 9/16-inch white colored screws.

Check how the door slides. If the door is hard to push—it should glide easily—or is not parallel with the side jamb, you can make adjustments. Located on the outside of the bottom rail are two adjusting sockets. Simply remove caps, insert a screwdriver and turn to raise or lower door as required.

Finally, finish off the areas around the outside and the inside of the door.

BUILDING PATIOS

Patio in bad shape? Don't have one? Pick and build from the variety here.

Super-simple patio? Log slices laid on earth.

Flagstone, patio-block and brick patio are favorite do-it-yourself projects. Following are instructions on building these and a couple of others to suit your needs.

BRICK ON SAND

This is a simple patio to build. No drainage pitching is necessary, nor mortar or concrete of any sort. A brick on sand patio is quite durable. If you live in an area where there is freezing, it is likely that the bricks will heave a bit as the ground swells from frost. In the spring, though, it's an easy matter to reset them, adding or taking sand from under them as needed. Too, they might settle back perfectly on their own.

Start the job by outlining the patio area with stakes and string. Then, using a spade, remove about 2-inches of soil. Break up the soil beneath with a hoe and rake it smooth, then compact it with a roller or compacter of some sort.

Next, you can install your edging. This is the material that is installed around the perimeter of the patio so that the bricks, which have a tendency to push outward, cannot. The edging may simply be 2x4 redwood planks, a band of concrete, or concrete footings with bricks laid flat in mortar on top.

Next, lay a bed of fine sand 2-inches thick over the excavated area. Then, start laying your bricks in place.

There are a number of patterns you can choose from with the running bond the easiest to install. It is best to provide a joint about ⅜-inch wide between bricks. Brick sizes vary and if you butt them you can end up with maddening misalignments and other problems. But slightly varying joint sizes can solve size discrepancies. To this end, it's also a good idea to first lay a line of bricks completely across the patio area, varying joint size as you reach the edging so you can use whole bricks instead of pieces you cut. Once this line is laid you can use it as a guide to laying the other bricks.

Bricks go on sand cushion. Tap gently but firmly in place using a soft-headed mallet.

When all the bricks are in place, pour sand in piles on patio, then work into the joints.

Various patterns you can lay brick in. The easiest and most popular is the running bond, right.

If a brick needs to be cut, do the job with a broad blade chisel and hammer. First score the brick all around by tapping it with the chisel. Then place the brick on a board and give it a sharp blow with the chisel blade pointing inward. A clean break should occur. If you have to cut a large number of bricks, you can rent an electric power saw equipped with a masonry blade or hire a manual cutting machine called a guillotine.

When all the bricks are in position, dump more fine sand on top and brush it into the joints. When you've filled the joints as well as you can, spray the area with the fine spray from a garden hose to settle the sand. Over a period of weeks rain will make the sand settle some more, so have some sand handy to fill the joints all the way to the top until thoroughly compacted.

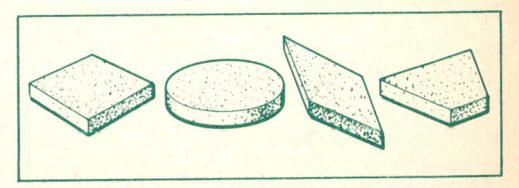

You can make patio blocks in a variety of interesting shapes, from round to triangular.

Key building consideration when laying patio blocks is get form level. Blocks themselves are easy to make, as shown in art on page 18.

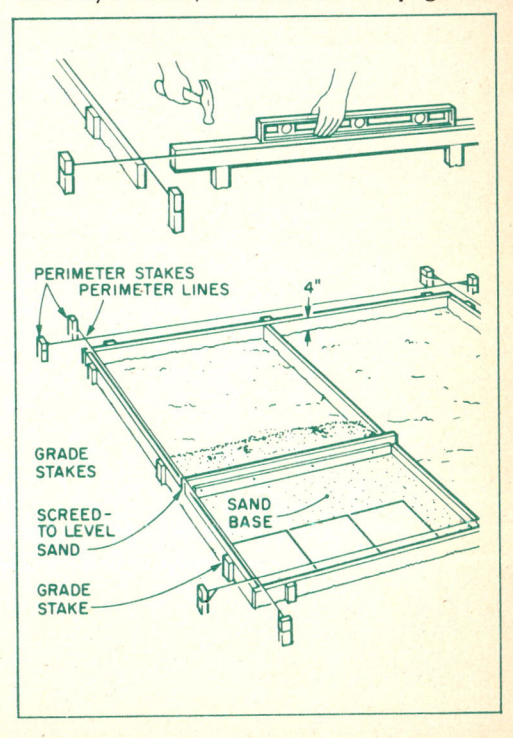

SAND . . . PLUS

If you wish, you can build a more durable version of a brick on sand patio, one that utilizes dry mortar mixed with sand.

Start this job by outlining the area of the patio with stakes and string. Excavate as shown in the drawing: a foot or so for the footings, 7-inches for patio proper.

Build forms for the footings with the tops of the footings sloped about ¼-inch per foot for drainage. Pour concrete. When cured add a 4-inch layer of gravel, then a 1 or 2-inch layer of sand or better, stone screenings or graded pea gravel level with the top of the footings. If the area is damp or shaded and likely to be damp, it's a

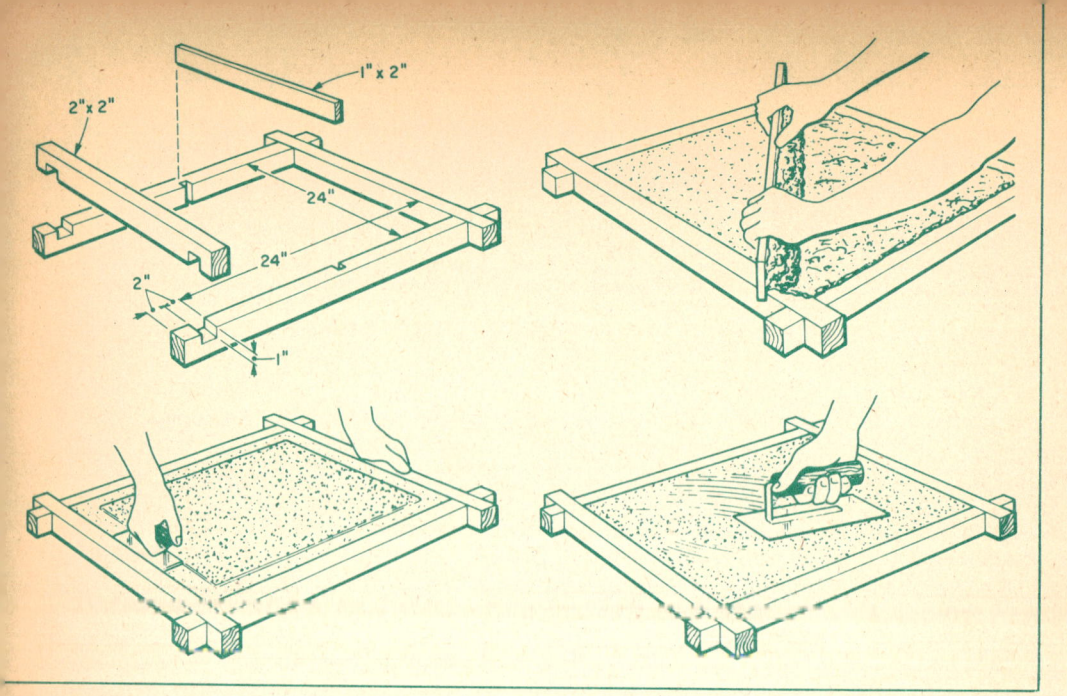

Patio blocks are easy to make with form you make of 2 x 2's. Text has all the details for job.

good idea to lay 15-pound roofing felt over the base before laying the brick; it also makes things easier on your knees.

Next, lay your edging on top of the footing in a ½-inch base of mortar, allowing joints between. Then proceed to lay the brick over the entire area of the patio as described above.

When all the bricks are in place, toss a mixture of 4 parts sand to one part cement into the joints. Make sure that the bricks are dry; otherwise mortar will stick to them. Of course this is no problem if you want a used-brick look. Sweep the cement-sand mixture into the joints, using a stiff dry brush and a small piece of wood to tamp it in solidly. (see above sketch).

When the dry mix is in place, filling up the joints, give the patio a spray with the hose wetting it thoroughly and taking care not to splash the mix onto the brick surfaces.

When the mix has begun to harden go over it with a piece of pipe or jointer to give a finished look to the joints. Wait a few hours, then clean the bricks by rubbing vigorously with a piece of wet burlap. After this use mortar cleaner as needed.

PATIO BLOCKS

This type of patio may be made with precast units you buy at a masonry supplies house, or you can make your own.

To make your own blocks, start by making a 2-foot by 2-foot form as shown, notching as necessary. If you wish, you can add interest to the patio by making some of the blocks only 1-foot by 2-feet (see figure). To speed the job, make several forms.

Grease insides of forms and set them on tarpaper. Mix premixed concrete mix, such as Sakrete, and pour into form. For added strength, imbed cut and straightened coat hanger wire in the concrete. When form is filled, level with strikeboard.

Smooth surface with wood float, moving the float over the concrete with light pressure in a half arc motion.

Round off edges of blocks and finish them with a steel trowel after concrete has set for about an hour (use wood float if you want a rough finish). As you move trowel over surface, hold leading edge up slightly. For best results, concrete must

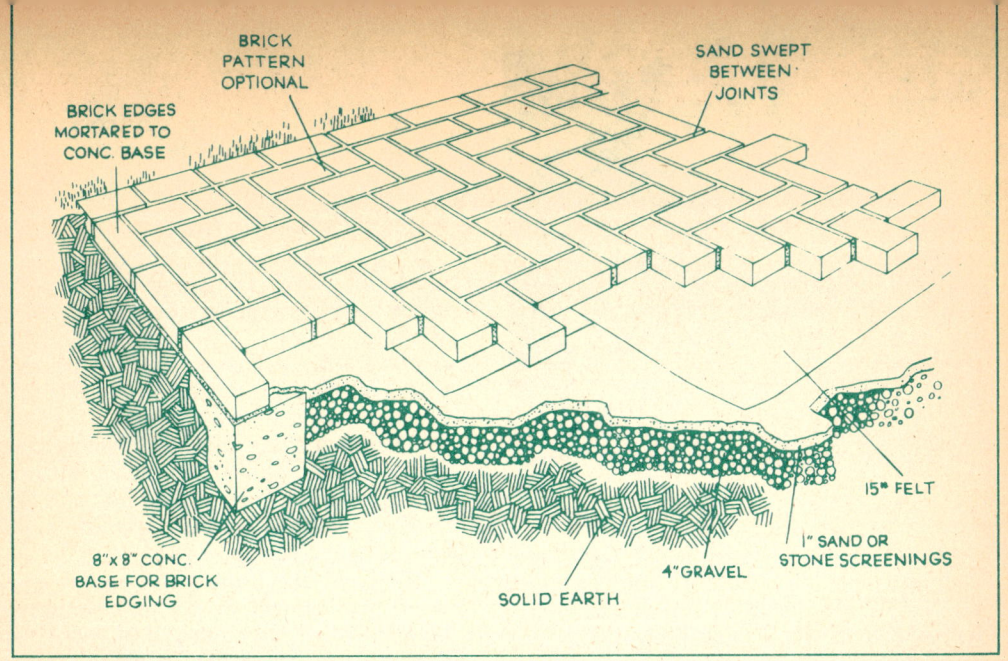

Brick-on-sand patio is simpler to construct than one on concrete, but will last for years.

be cured for a week. Forms can be removed in a day or two.

If you like, you can make blocks of different shape, or imprint them with designs. Just cut designs from heavy roofing paper. After troweling, when water disappears, place cut-outs on concrete; trowel over them to set flush—don't get too much concrete over top. Remove cut-outs 24 hours later.

Various flagstone patterns are possible, but you have to take care to avoid haphazard look.

multiple cut

irregular (fitted)

semi-irregular

all one size

19

Precast patio blocks are also available, and in a variety of colors. They go down easily.

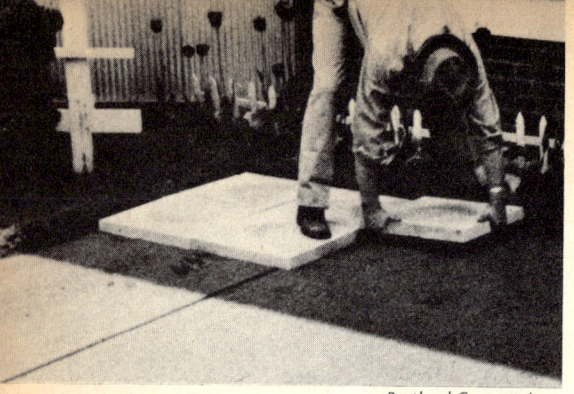

Portland Cement Assn.

One advantage of patio blocks is that you can make them over the winter at your leisure, storing them for use in the spring or whenever you do the job.

INSTALLING THE BLOCKS

To install patio blocks, first establish the perimeter of the patio with stakes and string. Decide what height you want the patio, then drive one grade stake into the ground about 1-inch inside one of the perimeter lines; the top of this first stake will then serve as your guide to the patio top, which is level.

Proceed to drive in other grade stakes, using a long straight board and carpenter's level to check for level.

Dig the area out to about 4-inches deep (from the top of the stakes). To aid in getting the sand base level and speed block laying, nail 1x4 boards to the stakes so the tops of stakes and boards are flush.

Pour a sand base about 2-inches thick. Make a screed from a long 2x4 and piece of 1x4 (nailed to it) as shown. Using the staked-in-place 1x4 forms as a guide, level the sand over a small area, then lay two or three blocks. Level these blocks by adding or subtracting sand from beneath them. You can then continue the job, one small section at a time, using the laid blocks as a guide to level. When finished, sweep sand in the joints.

FLAGSTONE

There are two methods for building a flagstone patio—wet or dry. In wet construction you set the stone in a grout bed on a concrete slab. In dry construction you use only a sand base.

DRY PATIOS

First, determine the size of patio and lay it out with string and stakes. Then, excavate the ground to a depth of 6-inches. While the edging, as shown in the sketch, is not essential, it does make it easier to set the stone and it retains the sand if the patio is raised above the grass. You can use a stone edging, about 1½x6-inches or a wood edge, either 1x6-inches or 1x10-inches, which can be staked into the earth as shown. When setting the edging, take care to make certain it is level.

Wet and tamp the earth in the excavated area and fill with sand to approximately 1-inch from the top of the edging. Starting in one corner, begin to lay the flagstones on the sand base, tamping each piece with a rubber hammer or a block of wood. If the stone sinks too far, pick it up and place more sand under it. If it does not sink level with the edging, move sand under it. To check stone level place a straight board from it across to the edging.

When all the stones are laid, sweep sand into the joints. An alternate way is to fill the joints with crushed stone or decorative gravel. This can enhance the beauty of the patio even more.

One thing to keep in mind when choosing flags for your patio is that larger, thicker pieces will stay level longer than smaller, thinner pieces. By keeping joints to a minimum width, sand and gravel will more readily remain in place and maintenance will be relatively easy.

WET CONSTRUCTION

Wet construction is slightly more costly than the dry method. However, the wet method does yield a permanent, maintenance-free patio. The basic ingredients of this type of construction are a 4-inch gravel base, a 4-inch reinforced concrete slab, concrete footing to frost line around the perimeter, and the flagstone set in a 1-inch grout setting bed.

First, as in dry construction, lay out the patio string and stakes. Then excavate the earth to a depth of about 8-inches as shown in sketch. Then, around the perim-

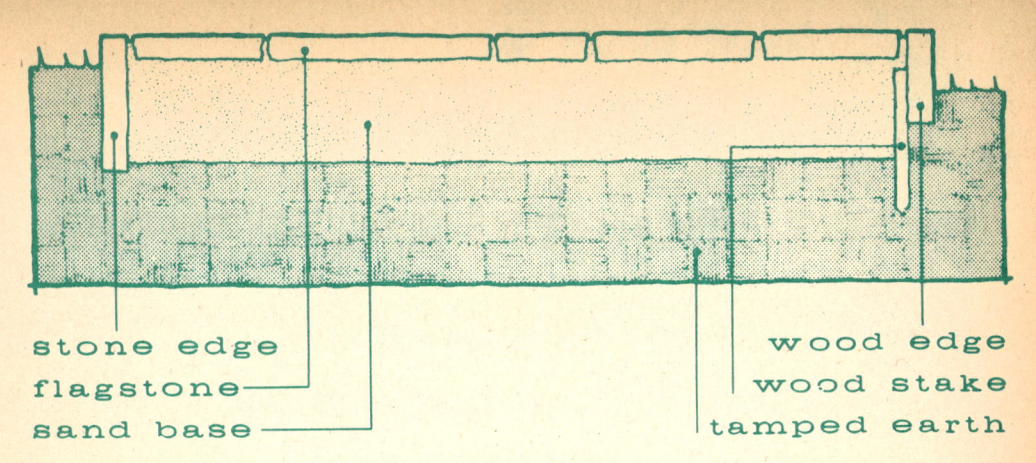

- stone edge
- flagstone
- sand base
- wood edge
- wood stake
- tamped earth

You have two ways to lay flagstone patio. Cross section above shows easier way, flags on sand.

"Wet" way to lay flags is on concrete base. A patio of this kind is virtually indestructible.

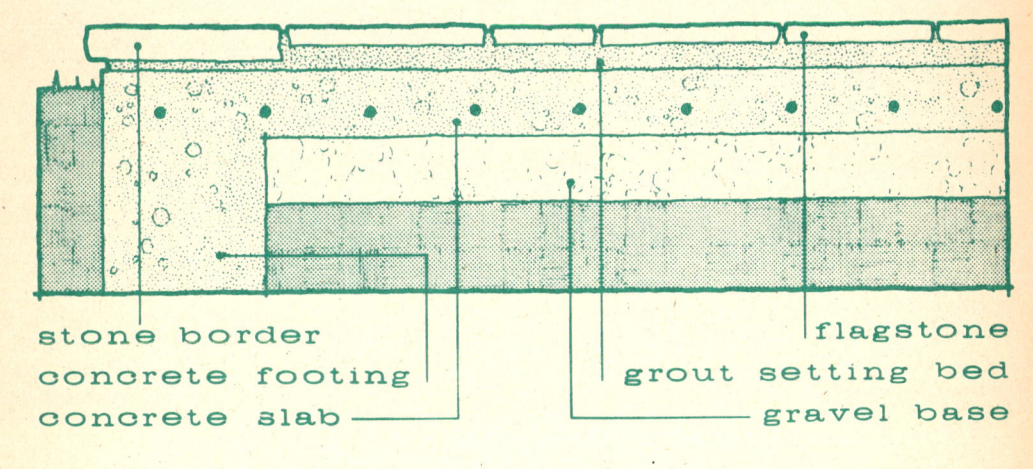

- stone border
- concrete footing
- concrete slab
- flagstone
- grout setting bed
- gravel base

eter, dig a trench the width of a shovel to the depth of the frost line in your locality. Some climates will not require a footing.

After excavating, set up form boards around the perimeter setting the top of the form where the finished patio will be. At this point, care should be taken to allow for drainage off the patio, so water will not remain after a storm. A pitch of ¼-inch for every foot will be sufficient for drainage. The form boards should be set to this pitch. Next, lay a gravel base in the excavated area leaving approximately 6-inches showing all around the form boards. Place reinforcing mesh wire over the gravel. Using a mix which consists of one part cement, two parts sand, and four parts gravel, pour concrete to within 2-inches from the top of the framework. Spread the concrete with a rake pulling the reinforcing wire up so that it floats midway in the concrete. No troweling or smoothing is necessary since a rough surface is desirable to provide a firm bond for the grout.

After letting the concrete slab harden (at least 24 hours) mix a grout consisting of one part cement and three parts sand with water to a consistency that could be balled and thrown like a snowball. Spread over the concrete approximately 1-inch thick as you lay stones. Spread only enough mortar for one or two stones at a time and tamp each one lightly by hammering with a rubber faced mallet or block of wood.

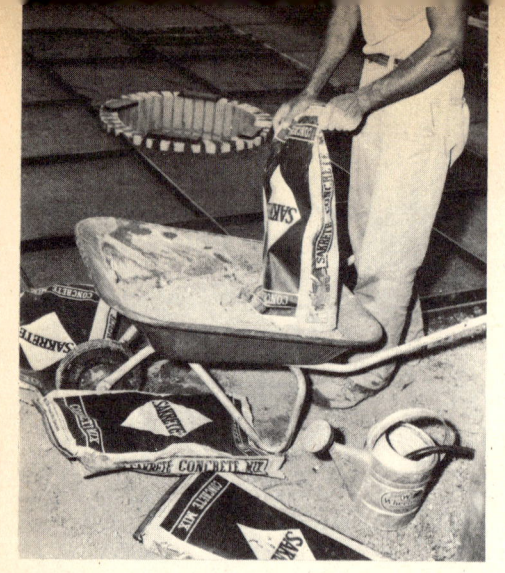

Premix concrete makes concrete work easier. You just add water to the dry ingredients.

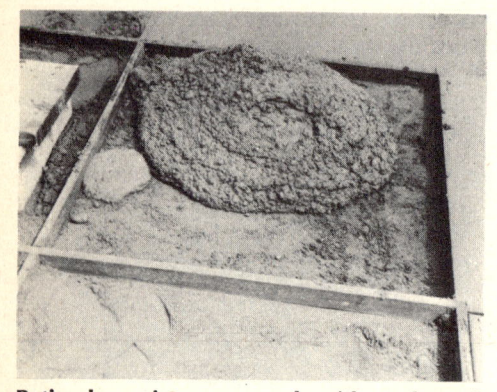

Patio here is segmented with redwood strips. This adds beauty, decreases cracking.

You can pour such a patio in sections, at your leisure. Leveling it is easy with a board.

Make certain each stone is level by using a long straight board placed across the framework.

After a dozen or so stones are laid, pick each one up and pour a mix of cement and water blended to the consistency of pea soup over the spot where it was. This adheres the dry stone to the fairly dry grout which otherwise would not bond strongly. When setting stones down don't attempt to fill the spaces or joints between them. These joints are not filled until after all flagstones have been laid and the entire job has been allowed to set at least overnight.

For filling joints, a mixture of one part cement and two parts sand should be mixed to a consistency a little wetter than the setting bed. Use a pointing tool to pack the joints tightly. Use care not to smear cement over the flagstone. If cement does get on the stones, it should be washed off, using a sponge and water, as soon as possible.

WOOD BLOCK PAVING

The idea of paving a patio or a walkway with disks cut from a log is a good idea—if you have a big log and happen to own one of the bigger chain saws. But here's the answer when you don't . . .

Cut the disks at a slight angle, producing oval shapes, instead of round. This way, even light saws, such as the Homelite XL2 will give you disks about 10x15 inches. And, the resulting paved surface is all the more interesting.

Before you lay the disks, it is best to let them dry, then treat them with a wood preservative. Since you cut them to a uniform thickness, laying them is easy.

First, make the base smooth and level. Then, spread a layer of sand and very fine gravel ("pea gravel") about an inch thick. Lay the disks in this bed, adding a little gravel or scooping a little away as may be needed to maintain level.

Then, fill the spaces between the disks with more gravel. The easy way to do this is to rake and broom a ridge of gravel across the area from one side to the other. Gradually, it will disappear into the spaces.

The next time it rains—or when you sprinkle the area with the hose—the gravel will compact, leaving just the right amount of texture to make the paving look its best.

Nothing drab about this slab when covered with blue-and-gold stripe all-weather carpeting.

DRESSING UP A DRAB SLAB

If the patio slab simply has the blahs, you can color or cover it.

RESILIENT FLOORING

About 8 years ago a major flooring manufacturer came out with resilient tile that was supposed to herald a new age in flooring. The material was colorful, easy to install with adhesive, and weatherproof. The only problem was that it didn't work as well on the job as it did in the lab (it came up, faded, etc) and was soon in disfavor.

Today, at least one other manufacturer has come up with an outdoor resilient flooring in roll or sheet form. It is installed with epoxy adhesive, and as epoxy is used to fuse the seams so moisture can't get under the flooring, soil can't collect.

The manufacturer, National Floor Products of Florence, Alabama, says that the material has conquered all previous problems. It is made of vinyl resins and colorfast pigments with a backing of fiberglass and asbestos and is constructed to last, and stay put.

You can get the product, called Unifloor, in two brick designs—a herringbone and a side-by-side, three-up pattern. Both are textured to resemble brick with joints made of a "vinyl sand" that simulates mortar. It comes in brick colors and white, and is available in sheets 6-feet wide. Installation is "relatively easy" the manufacturer says.

23

National Floor Products
Use resilient sheet flooring inside — and continue on slab to blend areas neatly.

SEAMLESS FLOORING

This gets its name from the fact that it has no seams. Indeed, applying it is similar to applying paint.

After the floor is clean and cracks patched, a white base coat is rolled or brushed on. While still wet you sprinkle colored vinyl chips on it. These embed themselves in the base coat in a random fashion, creating pattern and color.

When dry, excess loose chips are swept away. Following this, a couple of clear coatings are applied with brush or roller.

A variation on the system is one that uses colored sand instead of vinyl chips. The sand is sprinkled on the base coat. According to the manufacturer, Dur-a-Flex (100 Meadow St., Hartford, Conn. 06114) this is even more durable than the vinyl chip material. The people at Dur-a-Flex also say, by the way, that their vinyl chip system solves the one big bugaboo of seamless flooring systems: annoying maintenance. Systems with a clear acrylic top coating, they say, scratch easily, and dirt imbeds itself in the scratches. Dur-a-Flex's clear coating is urethane, which does not scratch readily. However, seamless flooring still has a nubby texture, so cleaning is not simple.

When a builder constructs a home, he rarely gives much attention to the patio. What you're ordinarily left with is a drab gray slab that is purely functional, with nary a particle of good looks.

This needn't be. There are a variety of ways you can dress up that slab, and without a great deal of effort. If you do, you'll be pleasantly surprised at the whole new look and feel it can give to the outdoor area —and the people who "live" there.

Before shot of this slab shows it as drab as can be. But seamless flooring face-lifted it.

First, the perimeter of the area was masked off and a cove material carefully applied.

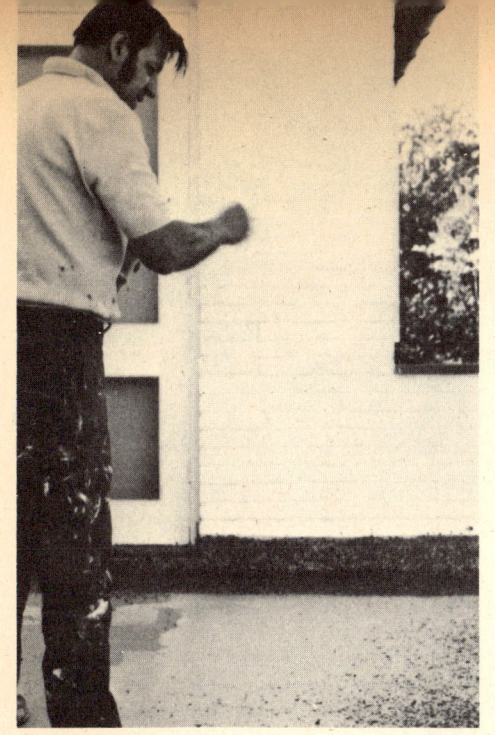

Then a white base coat was applied with a roller, and colored vinyl chips sprinkled on.

The chips form pattern and color, then a urethane coating is applied for protection.
Dura-a-Flex

CARPETING

Indoor-outdoor carpeting has been around for quite awhile now and is available in a wide variety of colors and styles. There is sure to be something to complement your outdoor "decor"—the style and color of your house and the surrounding area.

Outdoor carpeting is available in self-stick tiles or sheet (roll) goods. Tiles are 12 x 12-inches and may be installed on any clean, dry surface. Ozite's Colony Point line is an example. These, made of polypropylene fiber with an all-weather, foam-rubber backing, have a striped or ribbed look and are available in various colors, including gold, lime green and cherry red—nothing drab about them. If you install them on a patio, extra adhesive will likely be needed. Follow manufacturers' directions.

Carpeting is also available in sheets, usually 12-feet wide and in various lengths, and in set sizes, such as 9x12. This type is installed with adhesive, and has the virtue of having no soil-collecting seams. While you may want to cut the pieces to fit your patio, a set size may come in handy. You can install it just on the area where you set your lounging chairs and dining table and leave the rest of the patio—the part where the barbecue is—uncovered, or cover it another way.

Sheet and set-size outdoor carpeting are also available in a variety of colors. One type that is gaining in popularity simulates grass (This is the same kind used in the Houston Astrodome and in other sports arenas). While most people probably wouldn't want this as a patio material (un-

Elegant synthetic turf looks like it would be at home indoors, too. Wood strips accent it.
Ozite

less ardent golfers), it's a good choice as an accent material around pools and the like.

When buying outdoor carpeting of any type, read the manufacturer's guarantee carefully. While most types will stand up to wear for a long time, not all will stand up to the sun—they'll fade. Some companies will guarantee up to 5 years against this, but some will not.

PATIO IN REALLY BAD SHAPE

If your slab is in really bad shape—spalled, cracked, etc—there are a number of things you can apply (Resilient flooring and carpeting may be used also). One is a thin coat of mortar, troweled on after a bonding agent has been used on the slab.

If you wish, you can color the mixture (more about this later). Also, you can get epoxy compounds which consist of an epoxy resin, specially graded sand or colored quartz aggregate. It comes in two cans. You mix the two together, then blend with the sand, and apply it with a trowel. Here, as with any patio slab redo, you must first prepare the concrete well, be sure to remove all loose, unsound pieces. Unlike the mortar, the floor may be used the next morning. Dur-a-Crete from Dur-a-Flex is one brand. The product may be applied as thick—or as thin—as needed. It will resist damage from most chemicals, grease, oil, gas—just about anything. For easier cleaning, it can be given a glaze coat, but this reduces the non-skid feature.

A cure for badly spalled or cracked slab: First, break up, remove unsound concrete.

Dur-a-Flex

With loose matter removed, deep cracks patched, trowel on epoxy-sand material.

PAINT

One of the old standbys for refurbishing or enlivening a dead slab is paint. There are three basic kinds: latex, oil-base and epoxy.

The latex-type paints are resistant to wear, but not as much as the oil-base types. On the other hand, latex paint has a low sheen, whereas oil-base is high gloss, more slippery underfoot when wet.

Patchers such as Concrete Patch, by Red Devil, are easy to use. Add water, trowel on.

You'd swear the above was a well-manicured lawn, but it's Lawnscape carpet. No mowing!

Probably the best of the paints for outdoor use are the two-component epoxies. These come in two cans that you mix together before use. Application is with a brush and roller. If roller or brush marks are left, these can be removed by brushing over or rerolling a few minutes after the original application. If you wish, you can tint the epoxy with a so-called universal colorant, because it is "water based."

Before applying any paint, it is important, as with any paint job, to prepare the concrete properly. Remove all grease, oil, wax and excess water. In the case of epoxy, you can apply it over a damp surface. Remove all scaling concrete and patch cracks as needed. One convenient product for this is a vinyl-formulation patcher that comes in a tube and is easy to work with and feather. It's stronger than concrete, too. Red Devil makes it. Follow instructions on the package for preparing the cracks for the material.

STAINING AND DYING CONCRETE

Another way to dress up a drab slab is to stain or dye it with color. A variety of products, usually powders, are on the market for doing this. Instructions are on the package. Usually, you mix them in specified proportions and apply with brush or roller.

You also should know that you can color concrete by mixing powdered colorant into the mix, or by sprinkling it on after the concrete has been floated.

OTHER WAYS

In addition to the above ways, you can also cover a drab patio with brick, flagstone, patio blocks or the like, set in mortar bed. Or even install wood, using it as a sort of paving. Instructions for installing the various masonry materials are given in other sections of the book.

It's hard to beat the beauty of a wood deck. And decks can be installed on difficult terrain.

Decks to Delight

A wood deck is a delight in itself and perfect for sloping lots.

Decks have three great advantages, other than the fact that they function as well, or better, than other kinds of patio areas.

First, there is the beauty of wood. Wood is a natural material that harmonizes well in a natural setting. On the other hand, it will look perfectly at home in a non-natural setting.

Second, a deck can be used to conquer problems that would be difficult with other kinds of patio construction. For example, if the terrain is hilly, an on-the-ground patio would require a big, tiresome excavating job. But installing a deck just involves varying post height to suit the ground slope. Also, what if the ground is far below the access entry? A deck can be built up level to it.

Finally, wood is an easy material to work, as long as you're careful about dimensions and use good tools.

Following is a variety of decks you can build. Collectively, they cover just about every situation.

SMALL 10x12 REDWOOD DECK

This small deck is designed to adjoin an entryway into your house; it can also be a free-standing platform, or combine with a fence or retaining wall. Garden grades of redwood—construction heart and construction common—are ideal for building it. Use the decay-resistant construction heart for posts, skirting, and joists—the rule is that heartwood should be used in contact with the ground, or within 6-inches of the ground, for structural members.

This is, ideally, a ground-hugging deck, the 2x12 skirting lying near enough to the ground to create a boxed-in effect.

The drawings show the use of posts to

Before installation on 10 x 12 deck, the backyard area had very limited usefulness.

California Redwood Assn.
After installation, a whole new dimension in outdoor living opens up. Unit is inexpensive.

SMALL 10X12 REDWOOD DECK

- BARK SIDE
- PITH SIDE
- ANNUAL RINGS

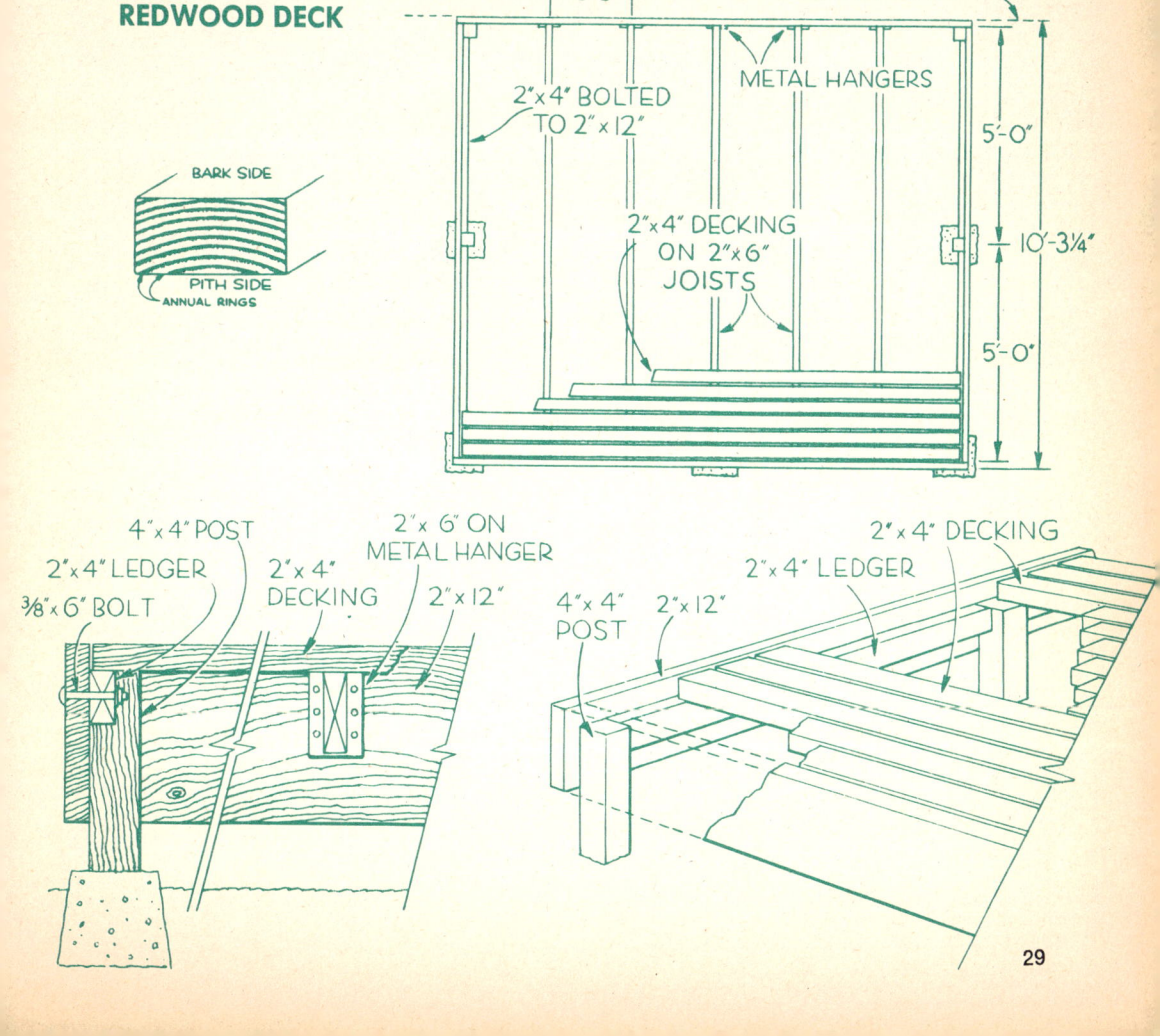

- 2'-0" O.C.
- HOUSE WALL
- 2"x4" BOLTED TO 2"x12"
- METAL HANGERS
- 2"x4" DECKING ON 2"x6" JOISTS
- 5'-0"
- 10'-3¼"
- 5'-0"

- 4"x4" POST
- 2"x4" LEDGER
- ⅜"x 6" BOLT
- 2"x4" DECKING
- 2"x 6" ON METAL HANGER
- 2"x12"
- 4"x4" POST
- 2"x12"
- 2"x4" LEDGER
- 2"x4" DECKING

29

Multi-level deck is not easy to build, but it is useful where terrain slopes. See detail below.

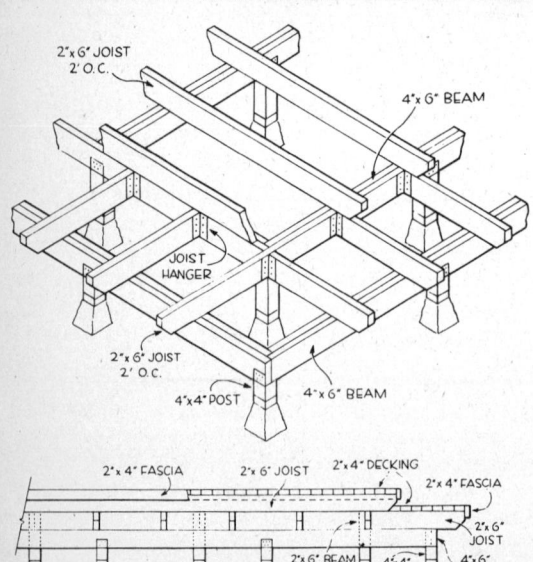

MULTI-LEVEL DECK

support the deck; posts may be necessary where the ground slopes or where the deck is to meet a high doorway. However, if the floor level at the doorway is between 12 and 25-inches above the ground, and the ground is fairly level, posts can be eliminated and the skirtboards attached directly to the footings.

Before you start building, apply a clear water repellent to the lumber. You can also apply bleach or stain. This makes a good undercoat. In addition, it will reduce the effects of moisture, and help protect the wood against dirt and grime both during construction and after. You can leave the redwood raw and let it weather naturally to a gray color.

DECK SITE LAYOUT

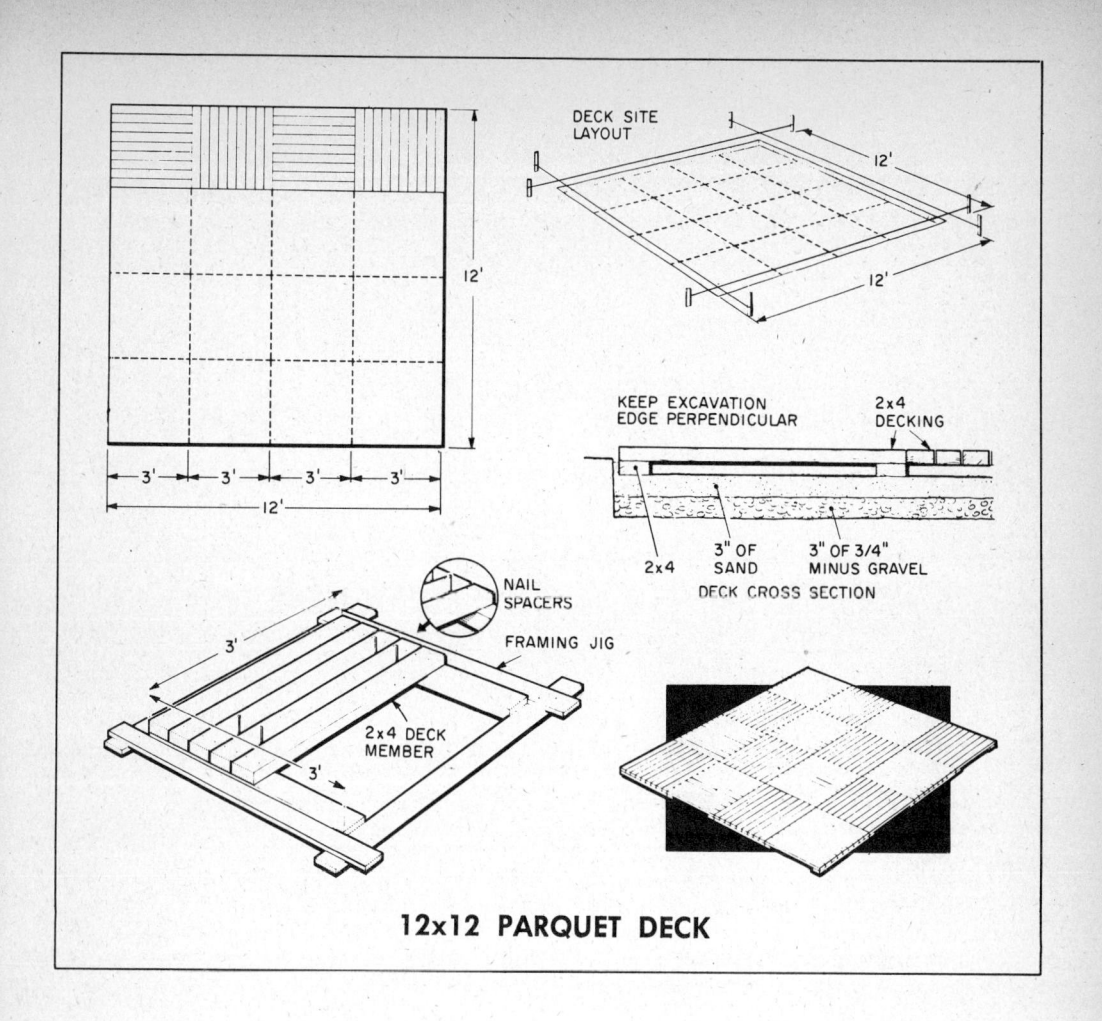

KEEP EXCAVATION EDGE PERPENDICULAR

2x4 DECKING

3" OF SAND

3" OF 3/4" MINUS GRAVEL

DECK CROSS SECTION

NAIL SPACERS

FRAMING JIG

2x4 DECK MEMBER

12x12 PARQUET DECK

First step is to decide the placement and height of the deck, relative to the doorway it will serve. The deck should be nearly level with the floor of the house, or else an easy step down from the doorway—that is, either 1-inch below the doorway or 4 to 7-inches below it. With the desired deck surface height determined, draw a line along the wall as a benchmark. This marks the top of the rear skirtboard.

Anchor one of the 12-foot skirtboards to the house studs or concrete foundation with the simplest anchoring system permitted by local building codes—such as 6-inch lag screws into the studs or expansion bolts into holes drilled in the concrete.

With the rear skirtboard attached, the deck's outlines can be projected from it by establishing a right angle from the house and measuring 10-feet 3¼-inches outward to where one corner of the deck will extend. Mark this corner with a wooden stake. Establish the other outside corner and mark it with a stake. Prove squareness of the projections by measuring between stakes, and between stakes and the house. Then measure diagonally between the farthest corners. If these latter measurements are equal, the corners of the deck are properly marked.

With corners and squareness established, five footings of precast concrete should be firmly seated.

31

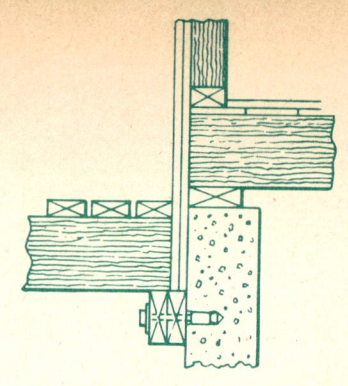

Where deck meets house, it should be supported by ledger boards. Two methods, above.

If posts are used, post lengths will vary with the unevenness of the ground. Accurate measurement of the posts can be achieved by extending a board out from the anchored skirtboard and even with its top, leveling it with the aid of a carpenter's level, and measuring the height from the top of the footing to the top edge of the board. Now subtract 1⅝-inches from this measurement and cut the post to that length.

Attach skirtboards to posts with ⅜ x 6-inch lag screws, and toenail posts to the nailing blocks in the footings. If posts are not used, measure from the bottom of the leveled skirtboard to the ground to determine how deeply to seat the footings.

With the skirtboards level and in place, nail them together with 16d nails. Pre-drill all nail holes near the ends of pieces to prevent splitting the wood.

Using metal joist hangers, attach the five 2x6 joists on 2-foot centers, 1⅝-inches below the tops of the skirtboards. Bolt 2x4 ledgerboards along each of the 10-foot skirtboards, 1⅝-inches below their tops. (If posts are used, the ledgerboards should be cut to fit between them.)

Now lay the decking. The deck will accommodate 32 2x4's spaced the width of a 16d nail inserted loosely between them. Because the garden grades of redwood contain knots, any large knot should be placed over a joist. This may mean laying the decking down loosely on a trial basis to check the best arrangement of pieces.

Depending on the cut of the millsaw, boards may have a vertical grain, which shows as parallel grain lines on the board face, or a flat grain (see illustration). Lay flat-grain deck boards bark-side up to avoid raised grain and splinters. Nail into joists with 16d nails, pre-drilling holes at the ends of pieces.

NOTE: Nails should be stainless steel, aluminum alloy, or top quality, hot-dipped galvanized to prevent staining.

MULTI-LEVEL DECK

This multi-level deck can be modified to meet varying conditions of terrain. Strength is important when building any deck, but it is even more important with multi-level decks. Before beginning construction, check local building codes for any specific requirements, weight loads, etc.

The deck is constructed with 4x4 posts on concrete piers, face-nailed 2x6 beams (net 4x6), 2x6 joists, and 2x4 decking and fascia. Members on, or near the ground should be construction heart redwood; all others may be either construction heart or construction common.

Connect posts to piers with metal connectors on wood blocks set in the piers. Beams are supported 5-feet on center (the piers are 5-feet apart) and are attached to posts with metal connectors. Joists are 2-feet on center and are connected to beams either by joist hangers or U-shaped connectors (when joist runs atop a parallel beam).

Set the outside piers and posts first, then attach perimeter beams. Alignment of inside posts is easier when outside beams have been set and nailed.

Once the substructure is in place and nailed, put on the decking. Lay out decking before nailing to insure proper spacing. Pre-drill both ends of each 2x4 to prevent splitting. Use only one nail per bearing alternating from one side of the piece to the other to help prevent cupping.

Allow ⅛-inch drainage space between decking members, using a nail as a spacer.

When nailing corners of the lower level (see illustrations), take care that a sufficient portion of decking rests on the diagonal joist so the nails will seat securely. Now place and nail 2x4 fascia along joist ends. Use 16d nails throughout.

12x12 PARQUET DECK

First, frame a nailing jig from scrap lumber with an inside dimension of 36x36-inches. Pre-cut 176 pieces of 2x4 lumber, each 3-feet long. Lightly ease the raw edges of each piece. If in direct contact with the ground the lumber should be pressure treated with a preservative, except if heart cedar or heart redwood.

Using jig, assemble sixteen parquet blocks. Allow a 7/16-inch space between the parallel deck members. Nail each end of the deck member with two countersunk 10d nails. Be certain to use hot-dipped galvanized, aluminum or stainless steel nails.

Lay out deck site with stakes and line. Excavate to a depth of 6-inches. Maintain a perpendicular edge and level bottom of excavation. Fill with 3-inches of gravel (¾ minus gravel or alternate). Level gravel with hand rake. Cover gravel with 3-inches of sand. Level sand and tamp firmly.

Lay parquets firmly in place, alternating direction of decking. When all parquets have been laid in place, fill outside edge of excavation with sand to ground level and tamp firmly to prevent parquets from shifting. Should you wish, you may toenail the parquets together for rigidity.

12x12 HEXAGONAL DECK

Lay out deck dimensions according to plan and locate pier positions. Excavate pier holes to firm soil as required by building codes. Level bottom of holes and fill with gravel to raise piers to desired height. To check pier height, lay 12-foot stringer between piers and check with level.

When all piers are equal height, place 12-foot stringer in position. Cut and fit 6-foot stringers and toenail them with 10d nails to 12-foot stringer at center pier. Use temporary bracing to position stringers in correct alignment. Cut and apply fascia. Cut and apply stringers "B."

Drive bracing stakes into ground and nail to stringers to anchor deck firmly into position.

Nail decking beginning at center. Center edge of first deck member over the 12-foot stringer. Use 10d nail for spacing guide between deck members, and apply remaining decking. Nail decking to each stringer with two 10d nails. Countersink nails. Check alignment every five or six boards. Adjust alignment by increasing or decreasing width between deck members.

Tack trim guide in place and trim edges allowing 2-inch overhang. Ease edges with wood rasp or file.

12x12 RAISED DECK

Follow dimensions in drawings to locate position of pier blocks. Install pier blocks by digging down to solid ground, leveling bottom of hole, dropping in block and surrounding with gravel.

Locate 2x4 framing studs beneath house siding. Drill holes through face plate and into studs at one end of face plate and then into every fourth stud. Attach nailing ribbon to face plate with 16d galvanized nails, two at a time, at 16-inch intervals. (NOTE: With beveled siding, use firring strips between face plate and house)

Raise three posts and brace in position. Install beam and toenail to posts.

Notch stringers and attach to nailing ribbon and to beam. Check plumb, level and measurements before nailing. Measure, cut and nail four diagonal beam braces in position.

Install decking. Use 10d nails for spacing guide between deck members. Nail deck member to each stringer with two 10d nails. Countersink nails. Check alignment every five or six boards. Adjust alignment by increasing or decreasing width between deck members.

Notch railing posts and decking as shown. Pre-drill railing posts and stringers and fascia and attach posts with two ⅜x3-inch lag bolts per post. Install railing cap with two 10d nails per post.

12x12 HEXAGONAL DECK

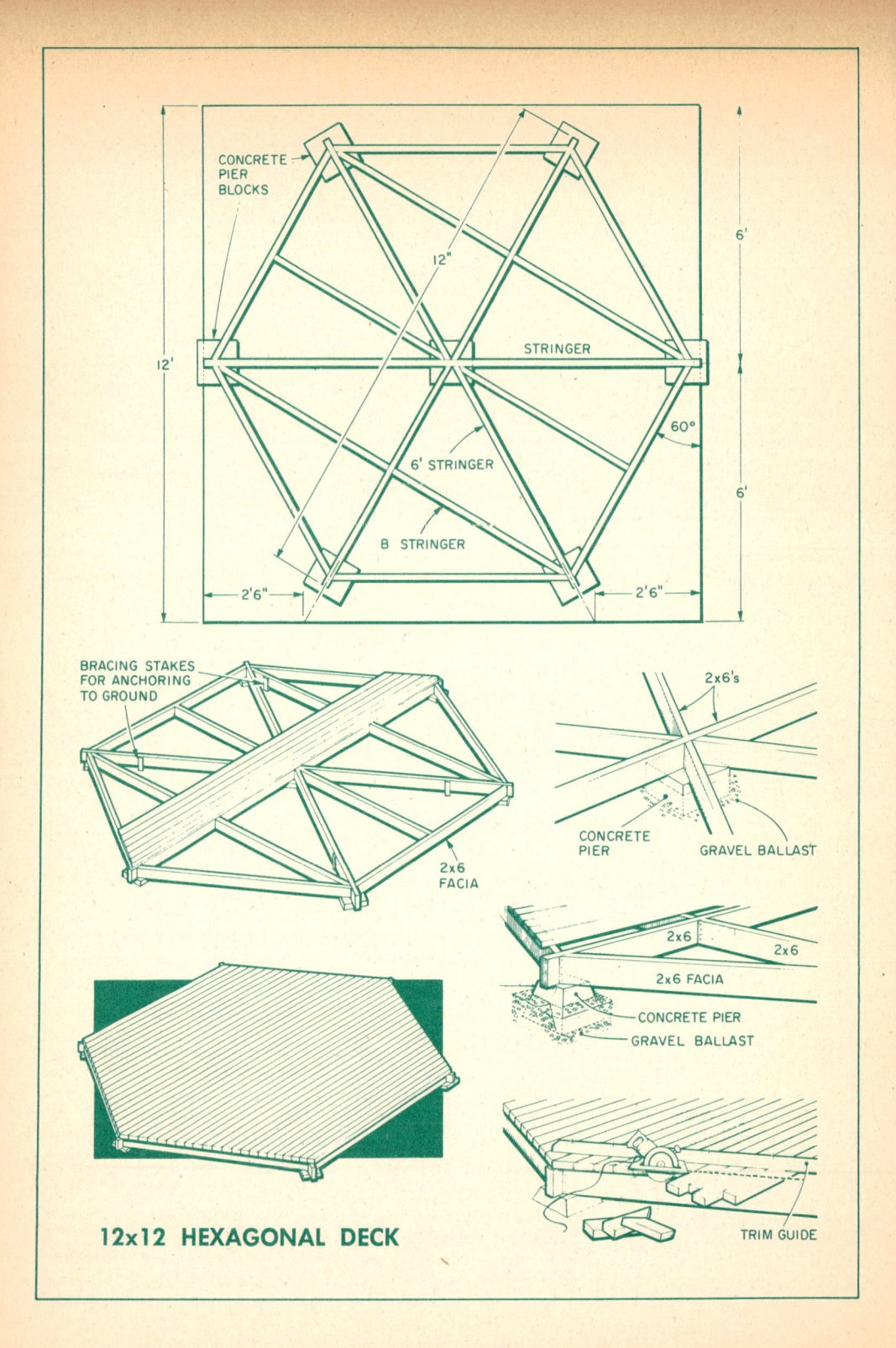

12x12 RAISED DECK

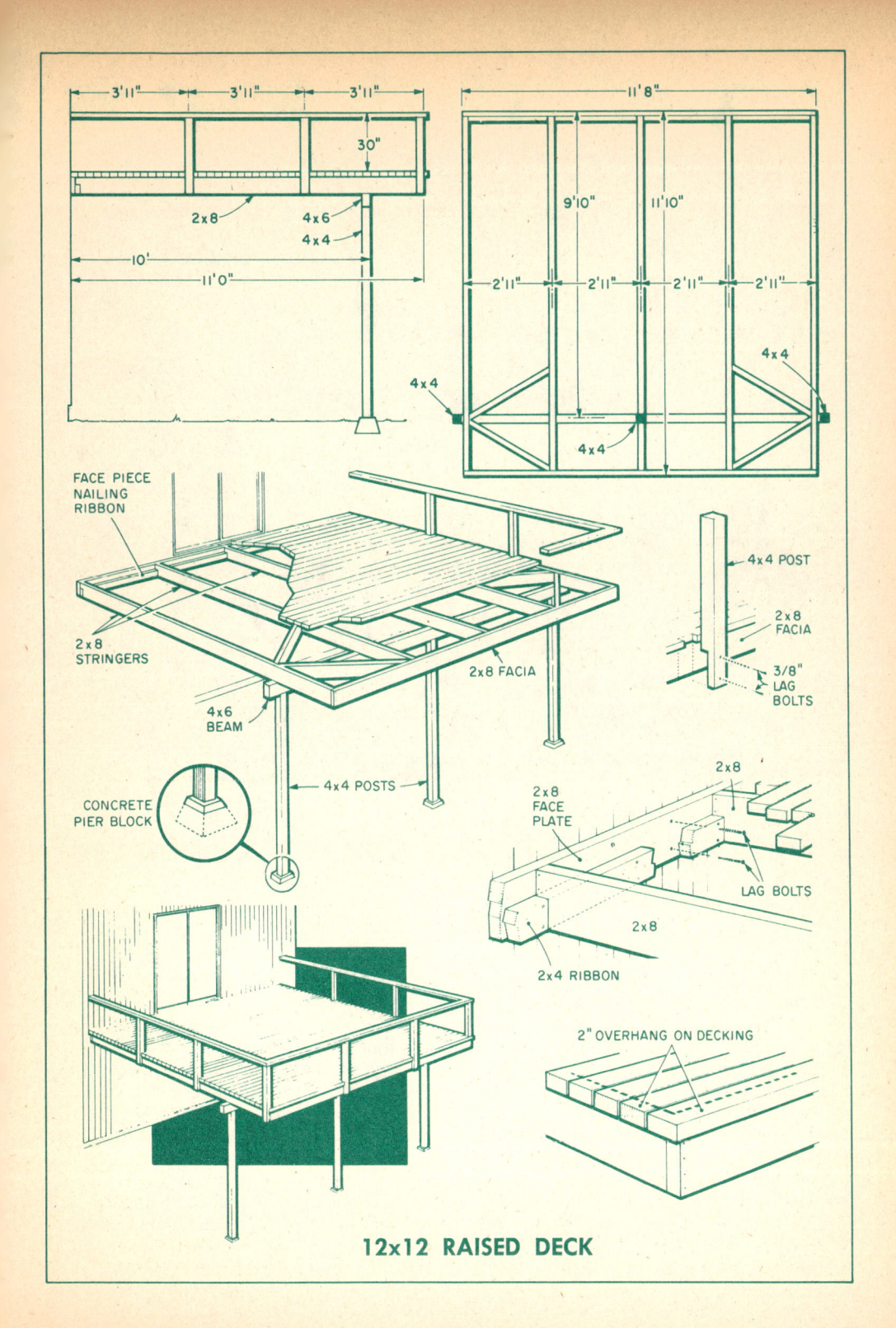

Filon

Fiberglass reinforced plastic patio cover lets a soft light in, but keeps much of the heat out.

LET (NOT) THE SUN-SHINE IN

If you just like some sun—here's a pretty way to protect yourself.

If you're the type of person who likes the sun—but in small doses—then you should think about some sort of shademaking or sunscreening cover over your patio. You can buy a number of types ready-made—including aluminum and canvas, but it's not hard to construct one of wood or fiberglass, such as shown here.

No matter what you use to build, be certain to allow some opening in the cover to ventilate the area under it. Even though the patio will be open on three sides, heat can still build up—and make things very uncomfortable.

FIBERGLASS-REINFORCED PLASTIC

Fiberglass-reinforced material does not strictly work by providing shade alone. Rather, it reduces the amount of solar energy, or heat, that comes through to the patio, but it allows a lot of light in, at the same time.

FRP comes in a variety of colors, sizes and shapes—flat, corrugated and ribbed. The lighter the color, the less heat that will come through (white is best in this regard). Also, you can get FRP in various strengths. Manufacturers provide information on how to support it. Most dealers carry four- or five-ounce per square foot panels, but those in heavy snow country carry six-ounces.

FRP is not for every house. You'd probably be better off using wood, or metal if you're seeking to preserve a colonial or rustic appearance to a house. Also, some codes, such as those in a "mountain fire district," don't allow FRP because it is about as combustible as wood. Therefore, it's not a good idea to start a roaring fire in a barbecue if the flames would come near an FRP fence or patio roof.

INSTALLING AN FRP PATIO COVER

The installation shown is Filon's series 410 which comes decorated with pin stripes and tape stripes. Cost is about 35 cents per square foot.

Installing the understructure starts with erecting the front header support posts. These can be either the ornamental iron variety or simply 4x4 lumber. Angle irons or post anchors will secure lumber to a concrete patio slab; iron posts come with flanges. The front header that goes on top of the posts is a 4x4, secured with T-shaped metal anchor straps.

The lengths of the lumber involved in this part of the job call for two people working together, as does the installation of the back header, a 2x6, on the house wall.

For protection from sun, a cover of solid boards.

HEIGHT ADDS COOLNESS

Getting a well-ventilated patio starts here: the front header should be at least 7-feet 6-inches from the ground, with the back header higher by at least 1-inch for every foot of distance between the front posts and the back wall.

Once the headers are installed, the man of the house can start nailing up the rafters, spaced exactly 2-feet apart. The outside rafters on either side of the patio are spaced just a bit closer—22-inches—to allow the side panels to overhang.

FRP covers can be as small or as large as your patio requires. Below, three choices.

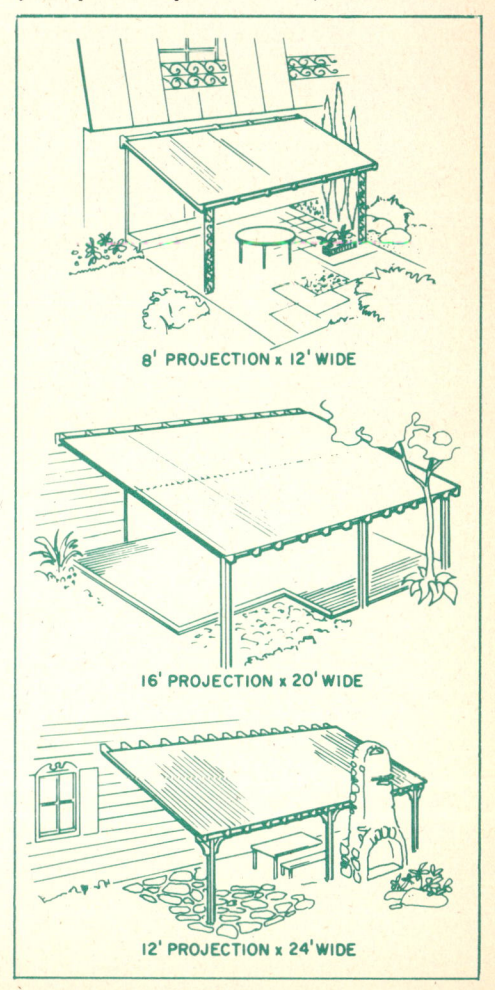

8' PROJECTION x 12' WIDE

16' PROJECTION x 20' WIDE

12' PROJECTION x 24' WIDE

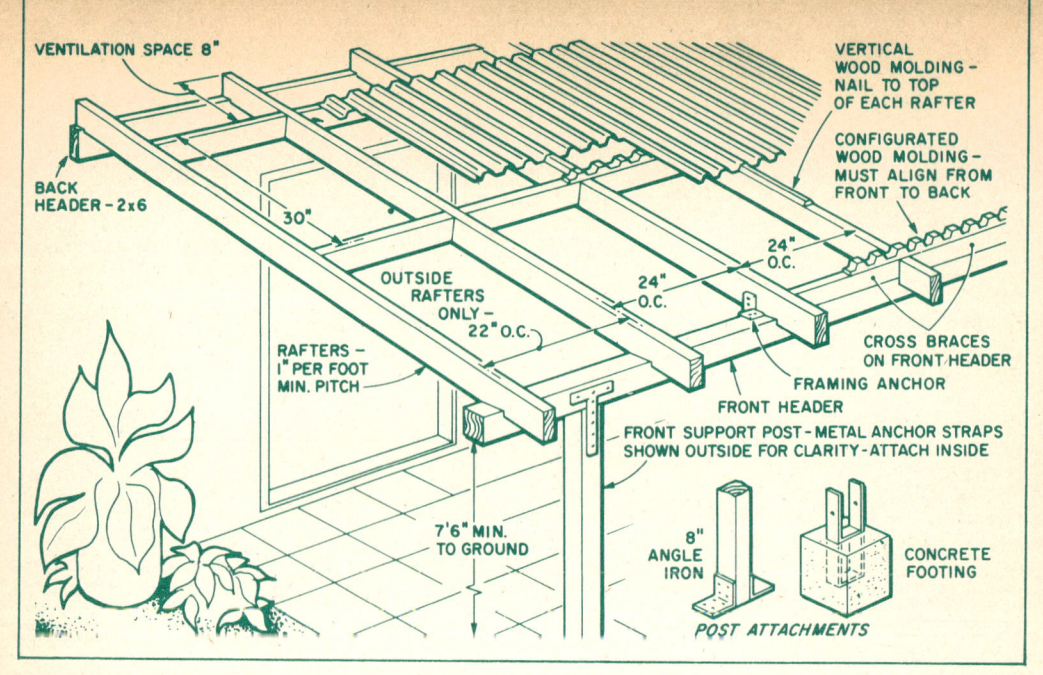

Cutaway view of FRP cover. One key construction element is to allow for ventilation.

Meanwhile, the lady of the house, if she's so inclined, can be getting the fiberglass panels ready for fastening to the framework. This involves pre-drilling holes for the nails, using either a hand-operated or electric drill fitted with a 5/32-inch bit. This completed, she can use a caulking gun to apply a bead of clear sealant along one edge of each panel. Pre-drilling nail holes avoids the possibility of small shocks developing when hubby wields the hammer. The clear sealant serves to protect overlapped panels against leaking joints.

If panels need to be cut to size, this is another on-the-ground chore that a lady might handle using a fine-toothed hand or sabre saw. But, since the panels come in a standard width of 26-inches and in lengths of 8, 10 and 12-feet, pre-planning can usually avoid the need for cutting.

CROSS-BRACES, MOLDINGS

Once rafters are installed, the structure is ready for the insertion of cross-braces, or purlins. These fit between the rafters and provide the basic support for the fiberglass panels. The cross-braces may be toe-nailed to the rafters or you can buy framing anchors to make the connections. Just make certain the cross-braces are flush with the tops of the rafters.

Installing the first row of cross-braces about 6 to 8-inches from the house wall will provide a ventilation opening at the back of the patio, where the open vent can be protected by the roof overhang of your house or, if your roof doesn't project that far, by a ventilation hood you can build with 2x4's and 1-foot lengths of fiberglass.

The next step is to fasten molding strips to the top of the understructure. These are 6-foot lengths of redwood that have been pre-cut to fit the corrugations of the fiberglass panels; configurated molding goes on top of the cross-braces; vertical or half-round molding goes atop the rafters. Now is a good time to paint or stain the whole understructure. Keep the color light to maintain an airy outdoors feeling ... a natural wood finish, a light colored stain or the same paint color as your house.

Install the panels so that prevailing winds pass over the laps of adjoining panels. If winds generally blow from west to east, for instance, you'd install the first panel on the eastern edge of the patio roof, lapping the next one over it.

ALUMINUM NAILS USED

There are special aluminum nails to fasten fiberglass panels. They look like screws but they're driven with a hammer and they have a cone of neoprene attached just under the heads. The neoprene seals the nail-hole against leakage. In particularly windy areas, it's a good idea to use special washers, metal bonded to neoprene, on the nails. These are much larger than the nail heads, increasing "hold down" and avoiding any possibility of nail heads pulling through the panels.

Nails are always driven into corrugated panels through the crowns, or high points of the curves. This prevents not only collection of water around the nail but also the danger of striking the panel with a hammer while trying to drive home a nail in the corrugation valley.

Posts are secured to anchors embedded in concrete. Ornamental posts can also be used.

A good connection between the posts and front header calls for T-shaped angle iron.

Predrill nail holes to avoid shock marks. Drilling can be done with hand or power unit.

Apply caulk to panels while they're still on the ground. It's easier than doing on high.

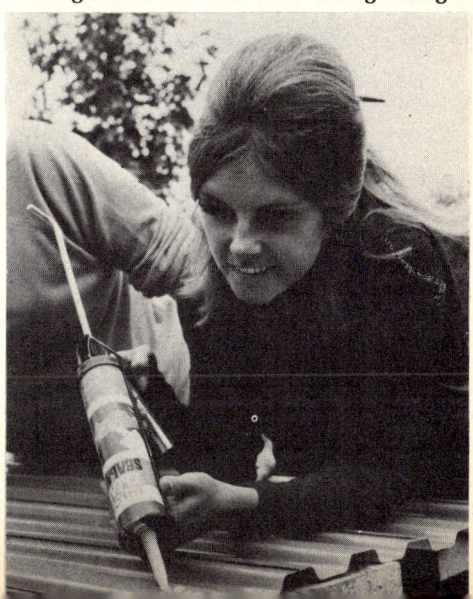

Start installing panels on leeward side of patio. Panels should overlap one corrugation.

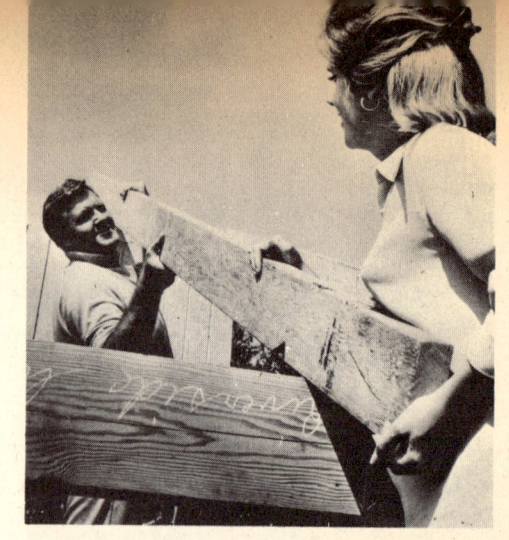

Raising rafters is definitely a two-man or one-man-and woman job. Precut boards to fit.

Cross braces help the panels carry loads (like snow). Space them all 30 inches apart.

Using washers with nails is recommended for high wind locations. Has more strength.

Panels themselves are light, handle easily.

WOOD COVERS

For natural beauty, it's hard to beat wood. It blends with almost any "outdoor decor." And, of course, is durable as well as functional.

Shown here are two simple but excellent sun screens you can make of redwood. Each is slatted on top, so you get constant

40

shade to some degree, depending on the angle of the sun.

DOUBLE-GABLED

Metal post bases are a key construction item here and can be set in any conventional patio surface. However, for best appearance, they should set over concealed double redwood 2-inch x 6-inch plates which support a complementary redwood deck. The double gables are for roof slat support and structure is tied together with steel rod.

Referring to the sketch, first set up posts in bases, tieing all together with temporary support boards. Install steel rods, drilling holes as needed. Install double 1x4-inch rafters. Nail roof strips on. Remove temporary support boards.

FLAT COVER

First, attach 2x4-inch ledger to existing structure. Set up posts using temporary

Cover above is more decorative than protective. But it provides some degree of shade.

Louisiana Pacific Corp.

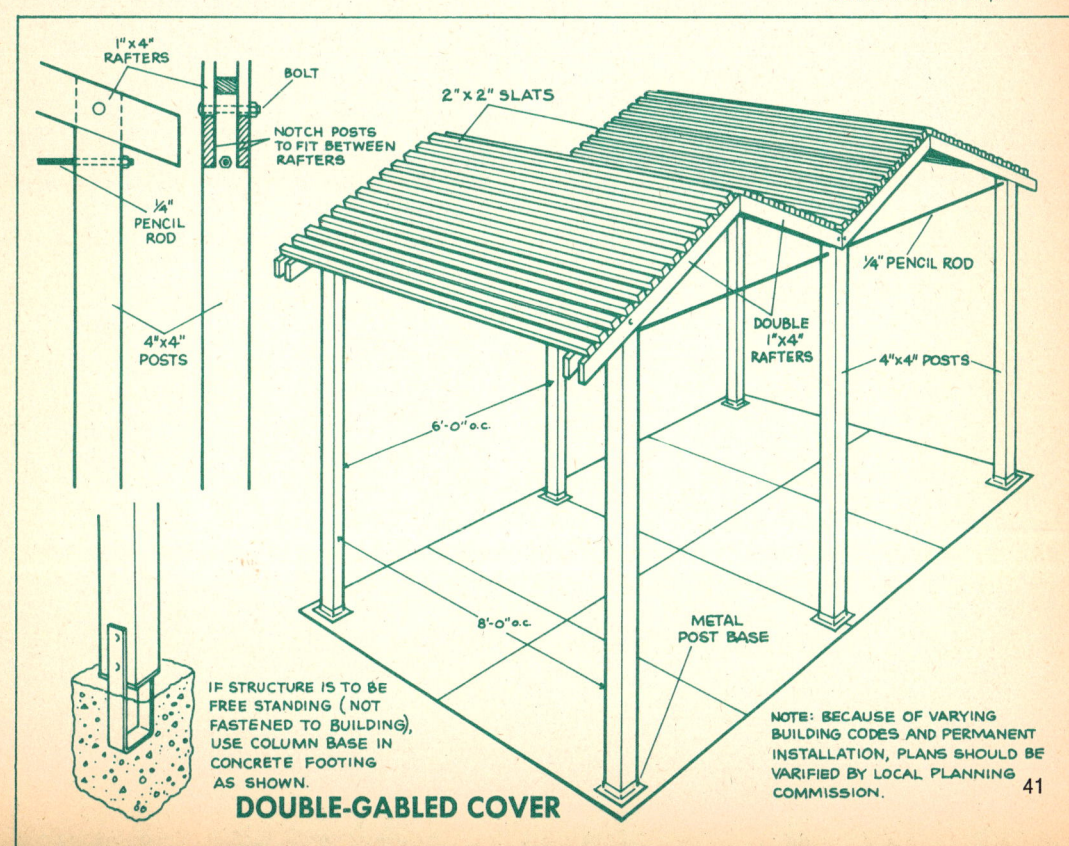

DOUBLE-GABLED COVER

41

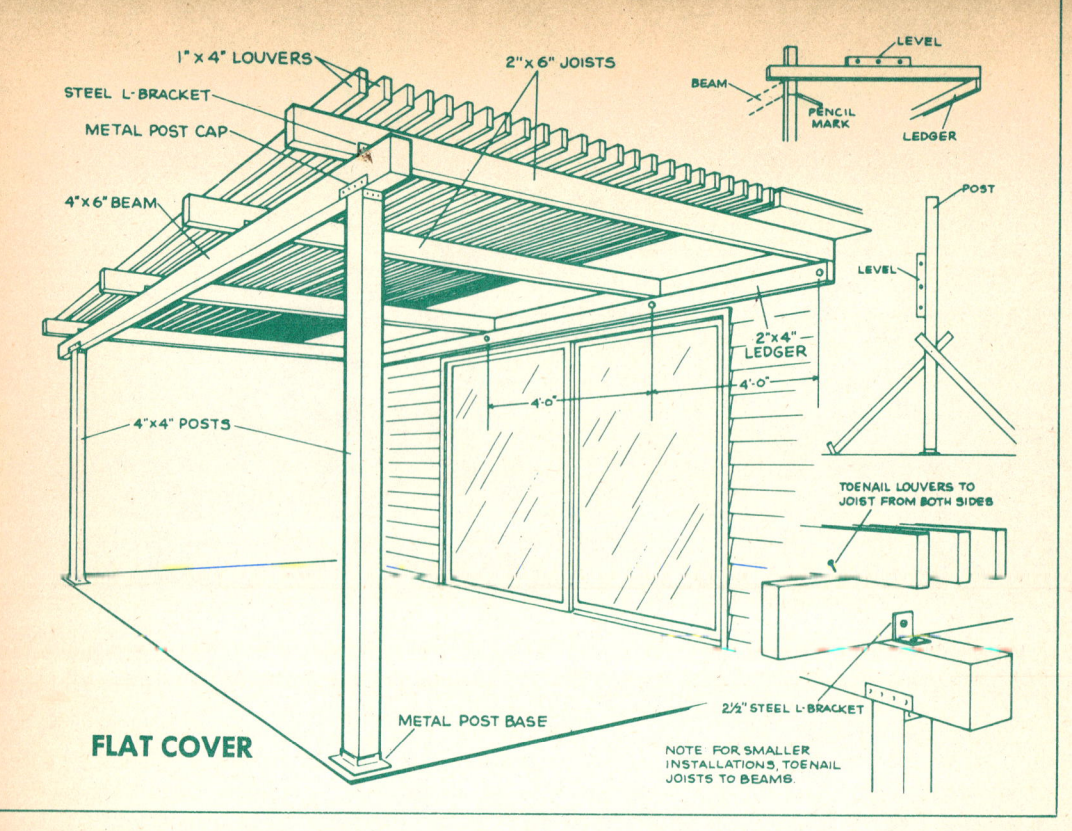

support boards as shown. Once posts are up, drop 4x6-inch beam in metal post caps, nail and place 2x6-inch joists over, using metal brackets for support. Last, starting from the side closest to the existing structure, start placing 1x4-inch louvers. For best stability of louvers, use a 2 by 4-inch block between each one directly over the 2x6-inch joists, nailing 1x4-inch to the block and toenailing it to the joist as you go. This will insure strength and even spacing.

For tips on finishing your cover, see the chapter on decks.

FLAT COVER MATERIALS LIST

Quantity	Size	Length	
2	4x4	8'	Posts
2			Metal Post Bases
2			Metal Post Caps
1	4x6	12'	Beam
1	2x4	12'	Ledger
4	2x6	10'	Joists
2	2x4	8'	Blocking Boards
8	2½"		Steel L Brackets
40	1x4		Louvers

Aluminum or stainless 6-penny nails

DOUBLE-GABLED MATERIALS LIST

Quantity	Size	Length	
6	4x4	8'	Posts
6			Metal Post Bases
30'	¼"		Metal Rod
64'	1x4		Redwood Rafters
50	2x2	10'	Slats
8		8"	Bolts
20'	2x4		Spacers for Rafters

Aluminum or stainless 8-penny nails for slats

OUTDOOR FURNITURE

Just like indoors, your outdoor living room needs furniture.

For enjoyment of outdoor living you need good outdoor furniture. If chairs are uncomfortable, tables too small, all your other projects on the patio will be for nought.

Here, we show you how to build both portable and permanent pieces of furniture. If you're like most people, you'll probably opt for the permanent kind. It just sits outside year-round and it is available whenever you need it. There's no need to carry it inside when the weather is bad. First, the portable type.

FOLD-AWAY FURNITURE

The portable furniture shown—lounge chair, high table and low table (which can also serve as an ottoman) has a special feature: Parts are hinged together, so you can fold up the furniture and carry it inside easily, and it occupies less storage space. If you wish, use them indoors. In this case, be certain to paint them colors that will blend with interior decor.

CONSTRUCTION

For the job, use ¾-inch, medium density overlay (MDO) exterior plywood. This type of plywood has an exceptionally smooth surface that's ideal for painting. If you wish, you could also use an A-A grade plywood.

Construction is basically the same for all three pieces. Start construction by laying out plywood panels for cutting. Use a straightedge and carpenter's square for accuracy. Allow for saw kerfs when plotting dimensions. Before cutting, lightly mark all parts for identification, then cut them out. Use a 1½-inch radius to plot the curve for all rounded corners.

Next, true edges with a coarse sanding block. Fill edges where required with surfacing putty. Allow to dry, then sand smooth.

Simple bench of 1x4 cedar boards accents deck, provides seating around three sides.
Western Wood

If table trays are desired, pre-drill, countersink, and screw tray parts together. Fill screw holes with surfacing putty. Wipe all plywood parts clean, then apply an undercoat. (Edges may require several undercoats.) Let dry, then apply finish coat and allow to dry again.

Now, you can start assembling the parts. To do the chair, use 3x3-inch lightweight hinges and first hinge the back to the seat as shown in sketch. Then cut aluminum angle (here, ¾ x ¾ -inch #3151 Colotrym aluminum angle was used) into 1-inch pieces with a hacksaw. Screw (with #8x

FOLD-AWAY FURNITURE

FOLD-AWAY FURNITURE

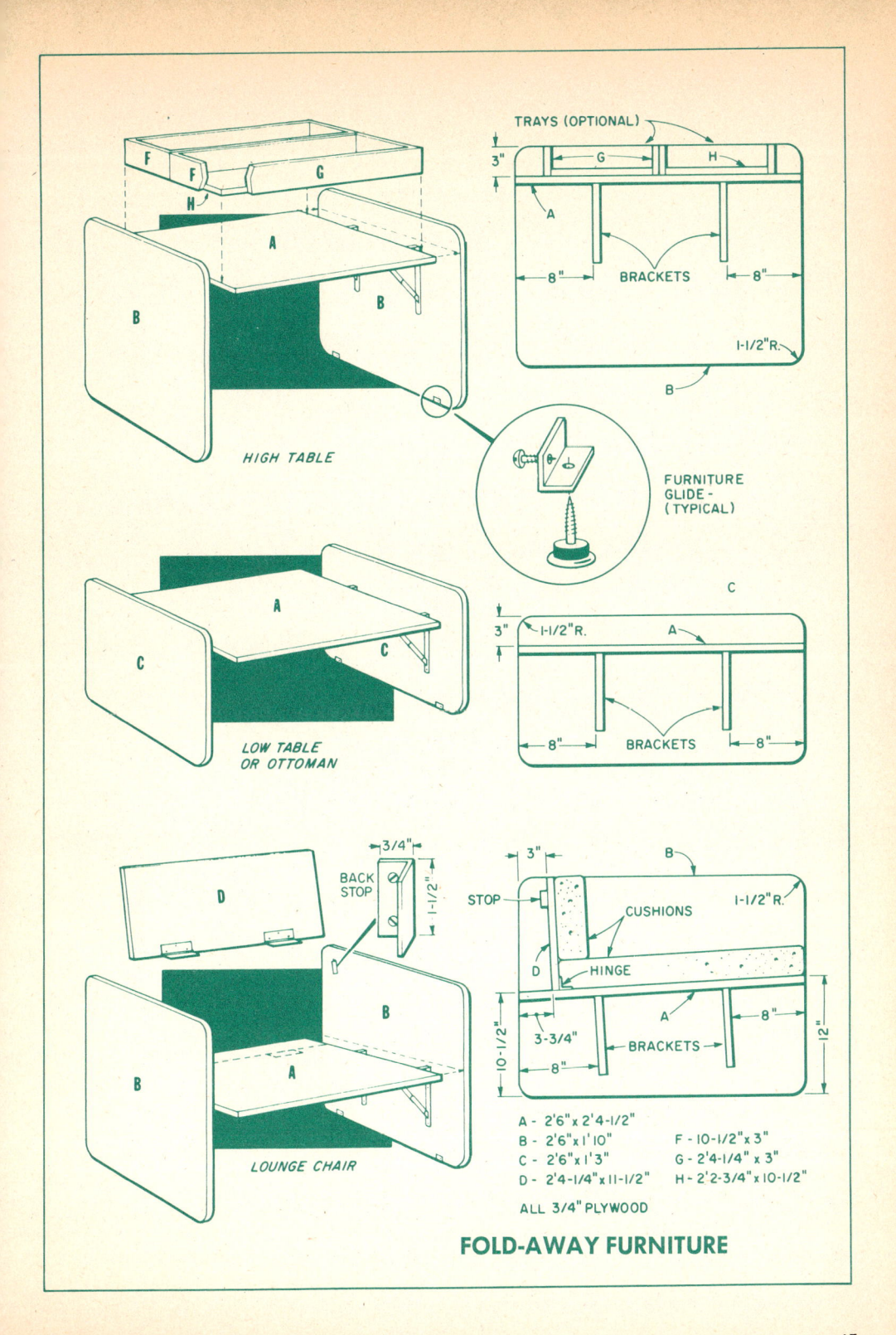

BENCH #1

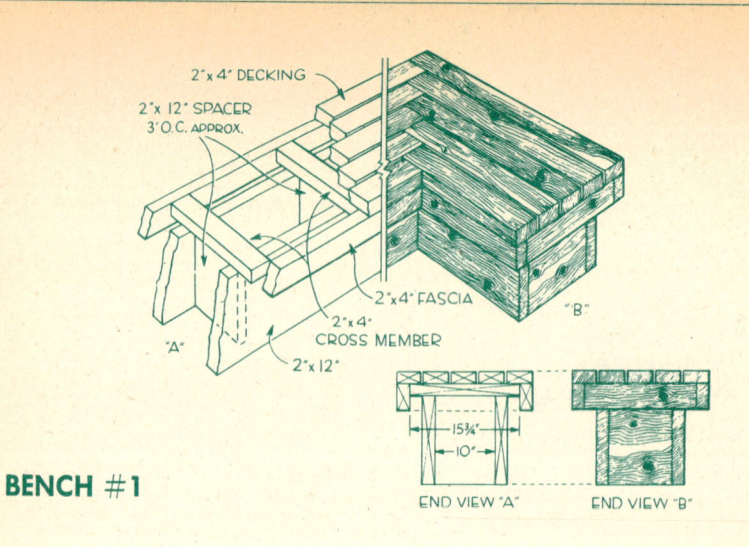

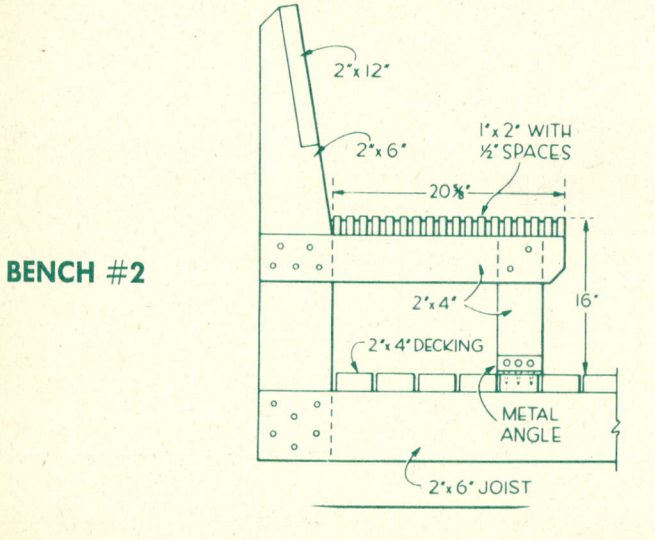

2" x 4" DECKING
2" x 12" SPACER 3' O.C. APPROX.
2" x 4" FASCIA
2" x 4" CROSS MEMBER
2" x 12"
"A"
"B"
15¾"
10"
END VIEW "A"
END VIEW "B"

BENCH #2

2" x 12"
2" x 6"
1" x 2" WITH ½" SPACES
20⅝"
2" x 4"
16"
2" x 4" DECKING
METAL ANGLE
2" x 6" JOIST

BENCH #3

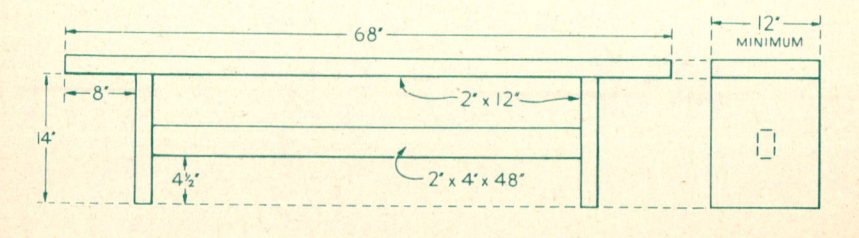

68"
12" MINIMUM
8"
2" x 12"
14"
4½"
2" x 4" x 48"

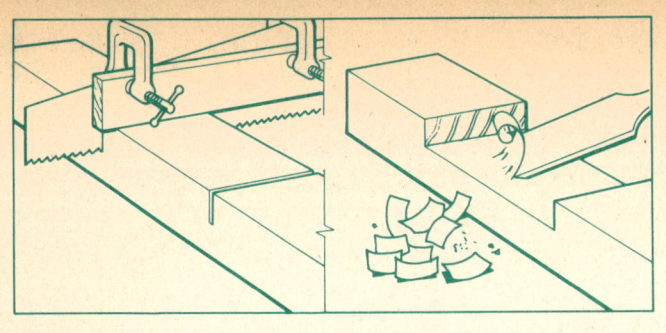

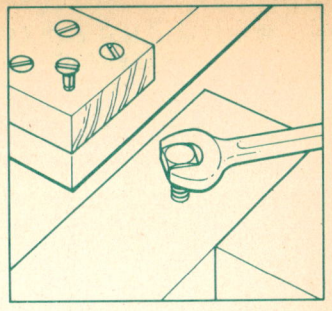

Joints should be cut with backsaw, chiseled out. Use heavy fasteners that will not rust.

¾-inch screws) them in appropriate positions with furniture glides (⁵⁄₁₆-inch diameter rubber cushion Bassick #CG 90 NE), then install folding shelf brackets (Stanley #794) with screws provided. Install back stops (1-inch aluminum angle pieces) on chair last using #10x¾-inch screws. If you wish, you can paint hinges to match the color of the chair. Cushions for furniture can be purchased to fit.

REDWOOD FURNITURE

For resistance to the weather you can't beat redwood in its natural state. The projects that follow are all made of this remarkable material.

TABLE WITH CONNECTED BENCHES

This compact picnic group is easy to move, always set-up, and ready to use, yet it takes no more space than a conventional table. It is also excellent for use with children because there are no benches to turn over accidentally.

CROSS BUCK TABLE

You're probably familiar with the cross buck table, but just never knew it by its proper name—it's the most popular patio table there is.

Small wonder. It satisfies most seating needs, yet is simple in design and simple to build. Although the dimensions given are fine, there's no need to stick to 'em. You can make the table in a variety of lengths by extending the top and seat.

THREE DECK BENCHES

A patio bench, by definition, is a long outdoor seat for two or more people: or a good stretching-out place for one. Aside from that, a bench can take practically any form you wish. Look through the benches here—you'll probably find one that you can adapt to your own patio.

If often happens that a bench can serve other purposes as well as seating: as a divider between one area and another, or marking the transition between a deck and a planted bank. A bench can broaden into a low platform, wide enough to function as both table and seating. It can be as simple as a broad cap atop a low retaining wall, or as intricate as an expert carpenter could wish for.

The most comfortable height for benches is between 15 and 18-inches—slightly lower if you are planning on adding a mat.

If your bench will be standing directly on the ground, use an all-heartwood grade of redwood for legs or other members coming in contact with the ground. If the bench is on a deck or otherwise off the ground, heartwood or sapwood grades are fine.

Bench No. 1 was designed to match a deck where 2x4's serve as the decking members (it can be adapted to 2x6 easily). As shown in the drawings, this bench is free-standing. With minor modifications, it can form the perimeter wall of a deck, or attach to a fence.

First, construct the 2x12 frame placing the 2x12 spacers 3-feet apart. These spacers determine bench width. Next, put together the 2x4 seating frame which will rest on the 2x12 frame. This consists of 2x4 cross members supporting 2x4 fascia. Space the cross members so that they fall on top of the 2x12 spacers. (Cross member length depends on spacer length and amount of overhang desired.) If the bench

MATERIALS LIST FOR CONNECTED BENCHES

Quantity	Size	Length	
6	2x6	84"	Top
3	2x4	35"	Cleats
2	2x4	65"	Bench arm
2	2x4	40"	Top and leg braces
4	2x4	34"	Legs
4	2x4	14"	Leg doubles
4	2x4	10"	Leg doubles
4	2x6	84"	Bench seats

is to be attached to a fence, nail the back seating frame fascia to the fence posts. If you build a corner as shown, be certain to place an additional 2x4 cross member diagonally across the corner to properly support the staggered seating members.

Now position the 2x4 seat decking on top of the seating frame. Before nailing, pre-drill both ends of each piece to avoid splitting, and nail at each bearing.

Bench No. 2 is an extension of a deck railing. Many variations on this theme are possible, and most railings can double as

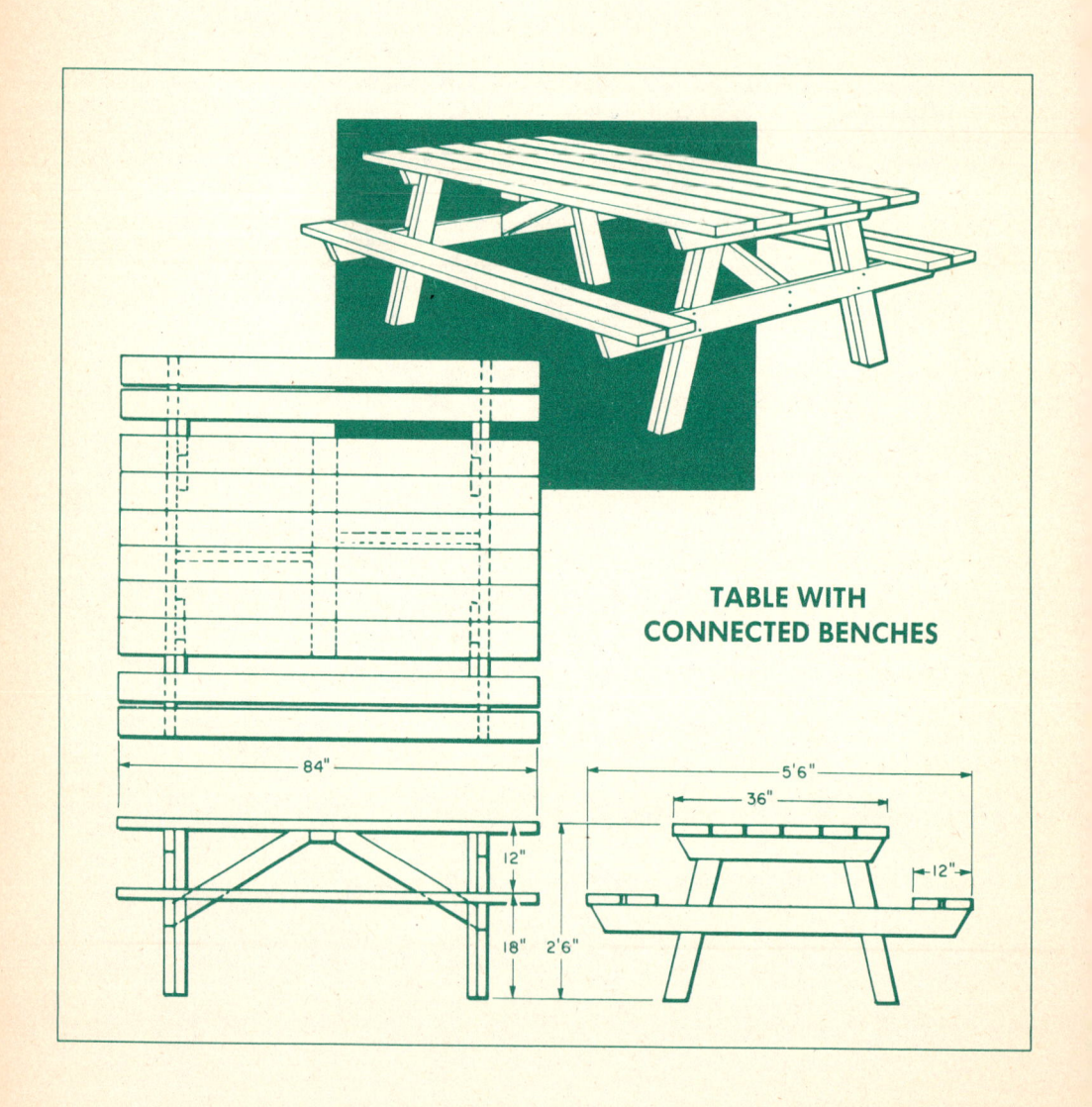

TABLE WITH CONNECTED BENCHES

bench backs with minor modifications. The seat slats are separated by ½x2-inch spacer blocks inserted and nailed every 5-feet. Bench supports extend from the railing's 2x6 posts (every 5-feet in the example shown), which are, in turn, bolted to deck joists and beams. The bench supports consist of pairs of 2x4's between which post and bench leg are sandwiched. Each leg is attached to the decking with a metal angle. Be certain your railing can support the bench and the strain of people leaning against the back.

Bench No. 3 takes only a few saw cuts and less than an hour to build. It's made from an 8 foot 2x12-inch (or wider) and is braced with a 2x4. Cut two 14-inch pieces from the plank's ends for legs, leaving a seat area 68-inches long. Center the 2x4 brace between the legs, glue with exterior-type glue (if wood is dry), and attach with 20d nails. Attach legs to top by gluing and toenailing from below. If unseasoned lumber is used, assemble brace and top with ¼-inch x 4-inch countersunk flat-head wood screws.

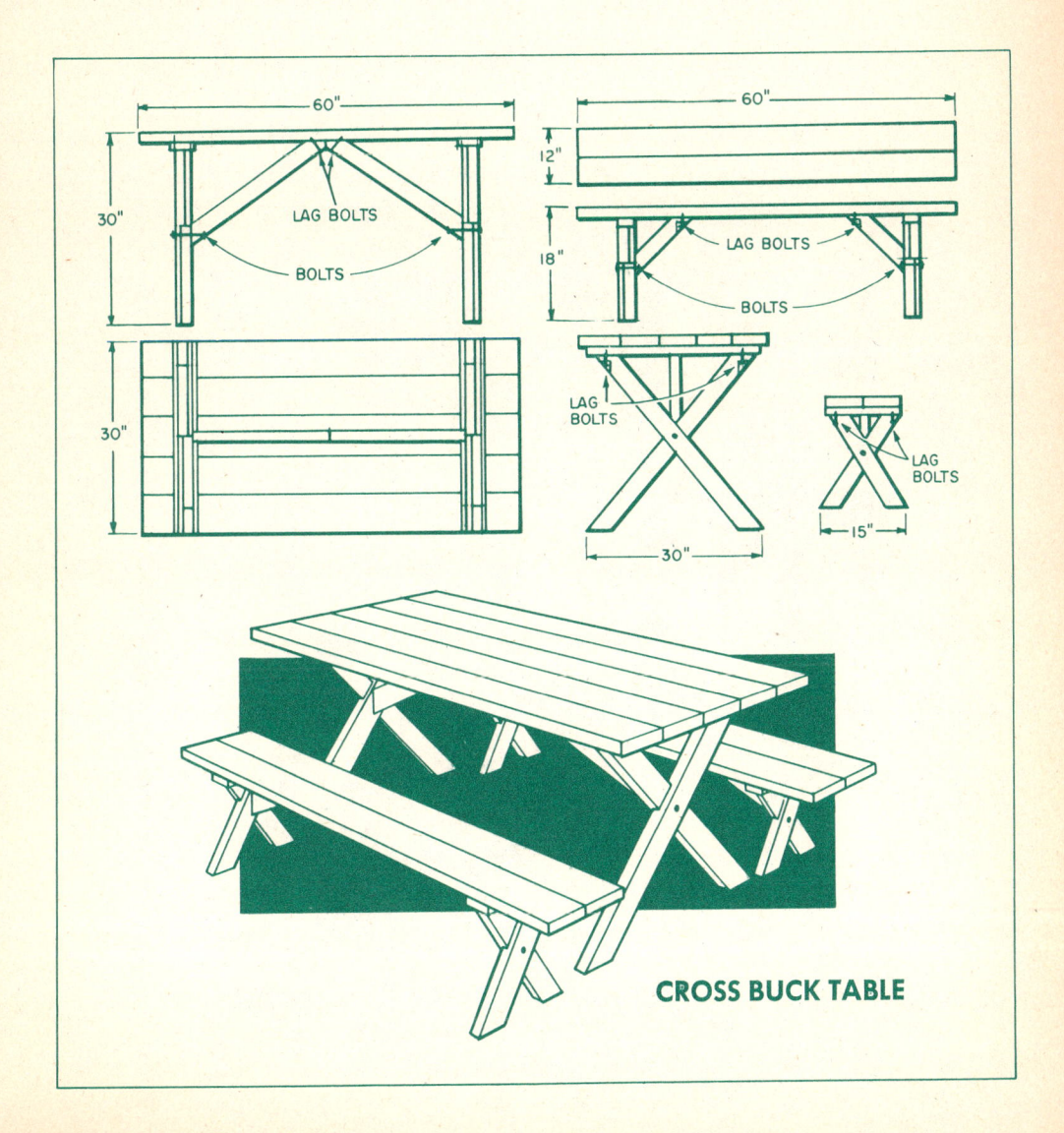

CROSS BUCK TABLE

BARBECUES YOU CAN BUILD

Built with or without mortar, a barbecue's a crowd- (and palate) pleaser.

To really get the most from your outdoor living area, having a barbecue there is about as essential as a kitchen is indoors.

There are many different kinds of barbecues you can build. We show how to build four kinds here: a simple brick unit, a gas unit, a pit type and a stone barbecue. Which you pick will depend to some degree on appearance, but also the amount of building effort you want to expend. Of the four, the gas unit is easiest. The brick is also simple. The pit type requires that a good-sized hole be dug; the stone one requires some skill at assembling the stone.

LOCATION

Whatever kind of barbecue you put in, you should locate it so it is easy to get to from the kitchen, not interfere with traffic on the patio; also the paths that lead to and from it should be solid—you want a sure-footed surface.

Gas barbecue comes preassembled. You build the slab, then make simple gas line hook up.

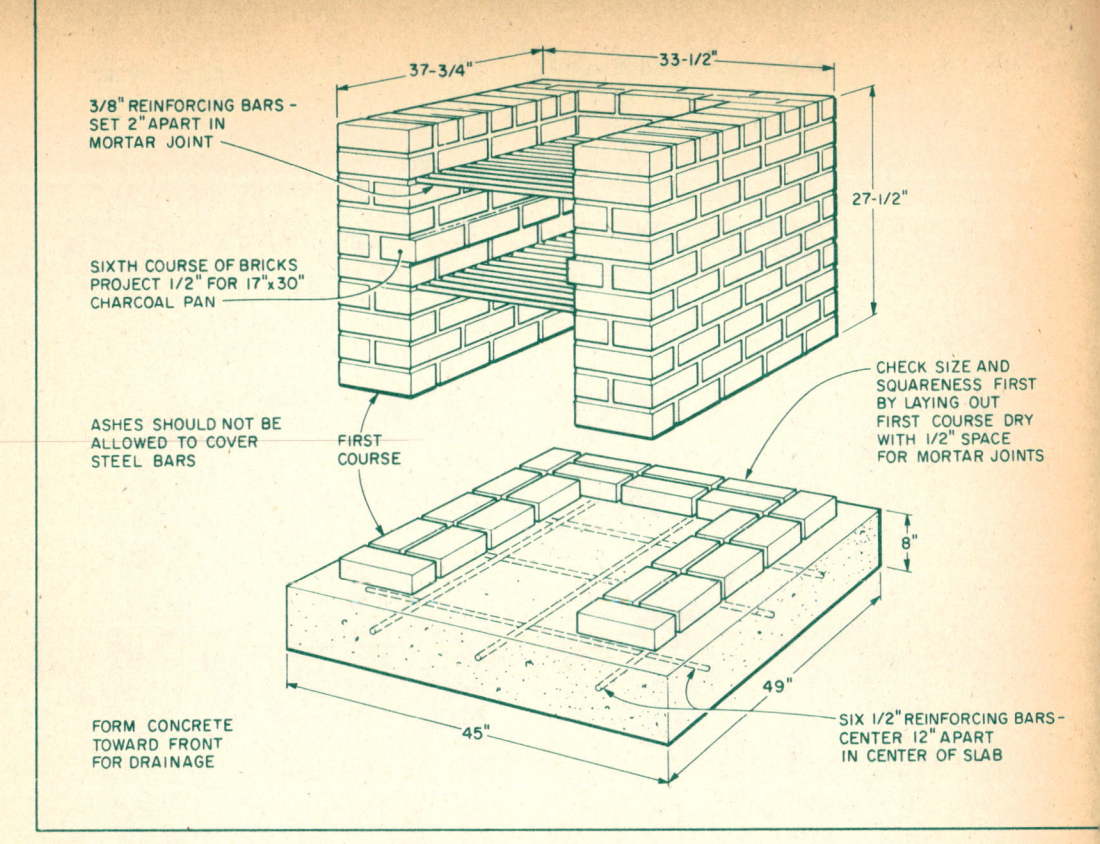

Classic barbecue is one of brick. Make sure that the slab it rests on is sloped for drainage.

BRICK BARBECUE

For this unit, which has an immovable grill and grate, you can use 250 ordinary bricks, and a prepared mortar.

Construction depends on what your patio situation is. If you have a slab, you can build the barbecue directly on it. If the barbecue will not be located in a position on the slab where natural drainage takes place, it would be well to mount it on a slab from 4 to 6-inches thick, suitably pitched.

If you have no patio slab, also construct a slab (See drawing for complete details). If the soil it is going on drains well, you can build it directly on the earth, after first wetting and compacting it thoroughly. In poor drainage areas, first dig a hole deep enough to accommodate 6 to 8-inches of gravel and a 6-inch slab that rises a couple of inches above the surface.

Following details in the drawings, and information for laying brick, construct the barbecue. Note that the sixth course of bricks on both sides of the unit are inset a bit to accommodate a charcoal pan.

GAS BARBECUE

The basic unit comes ready to install (and can be closed for smoke cooking). It operates on propane gas and can save you a lot of time and energy lugging and lighting up charcoal.

It's best to build this type of unit on earth. Built on a patio slab, you'd have to break into the concrete to mount a post that houses the gas line.

First, excavate the soil as needed to accommodate a 6-inch slab and gravel, depending on drainage, having previously marked off the slab area with stakes and string. Build a 1x4 form for the slab, leveling it. Find the center of the excavation, then dig a 24-inch hole there and stick in the post for the gas line. Plumb it with a level, then fill in around it with concrete and let set.

Following instructions for the unit you get, attach the gas line to the bottom of the post. When this is done, cover with a bed of sand, then fill in with concrete, level with the form boards.

The gas line at the other end attaches to a tank of propane gas. This, too, should be set on a small concrete slab.

Finally, install barbecue unit on top of post as indicated in manufacturer's instructions. If you wish, you can hide the propane tank by building it in behind a small planter wall, as we did.

1. First step in making slab for gas barbecue is to stake forms in place. Get them level.

2. Use a ruler to measure from edge of form to where center of slab will be. Dig hole.

3. Hole should be about two feet deep, from bottom to top of form. Use post hole digger.

4. Wedge post in soil, propping in place with stines. Then check for trueness with a level.

5. With post true, shovel in a stiff mix of concrete. Then check again for trueness.

6. Make gas line connection while concrete is still wet. Instructions come with gas unit.

7. Using trowel, pack concrete in around post. Make sure you poke out all air pockets.

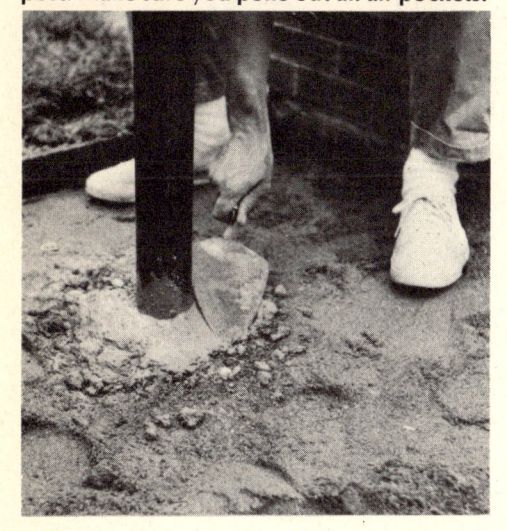

8. Smooth concrete with board for rough texture, use steel trowel for smooth surface.

PIT BARBECUE

This is an unusual type of barbecue, but it has definite advantages. The fire is about level with the ground. In use, the barbecuers ring the pit and use long forks to spear the food.

If you plan to install it on an existing patio slab, you'll have to break up the patio to the diameter of the pit you plan (It can be any diameter you wish, but about 4-feet across is about right). It can also be installed directly in the ground.

First, dig a saucer-shaped hole to a depth of about 2-feet. Fill the bottom 18

53

Cover-table for pit barbecue is made with redwood. Use angles at joints as shown.

Supporting pieces being pointed to also help to make unit extra strong, wobble-free.

Top of cover-table can be set on pit barbecue to protect. Use rust-proof nails.

Pit barbecue in action. Note cover being used as table top on right. Offbeat unit works well.

to 20-inches of this hole with ¾-inch gravel. Then fill the top 6-inches with pea gravel. Mortar bricks in a circle around the pit and you're ready to lay in charcoal and cook. Items wrapped in foil may be set directly in the hot coals. Hamburgers, hot dogs and other items should be set on a grill that fits over the pit.

If you are installing the brick directly on bare earth, it's best to first build a 2 to 3-inch base of concrete to set the bricks on.

When the pit is not being used, you can build a simple cover as shown in the drawing. This will not only protect the barbecue pit, but serve as a low table.

STONE BARBECUE UNIT

First, choose your grill equipment. The size of the top opening is determined by the grill and grate size. In this instance it is 12-inches by 24-inches, but you can use what-

To make pit barbecue, shallow hole is first dug, then a layer of gravel spread on bottom.

Edging for barbecue unit can simply be a couple of rows of bricks, either new or old.

Butter each brick completely with mortar, then tap in place and check for levelness.

ever size you feel is appropriate for your family. The height of the cooking surface should be from 24 to 30-inches.

In selecting stone for your barbecue, choose pieces that are generally rectangular —easier to install. Avoid the use of odd shapes.

A reinforced concrete slab about 8-inches deep is a satisfactory base for most standard-sized barbecues. In areas where freezing occurs, the slab bottom should be below frost line. The outside dimensions of the base should be about 6-inches greater all around than the outside of the barbecue. To make the base, excavate the desired area about 8-inches. Set up boards around the perimeter of the excavation. Place reinforcing mesh wire in the bottom. Mix concrete consisting of one part cement, two parts sand, and four parts gravel. Fill the entire excavation to the top of the boards, and with a rake pull the reinforcing wire up into the concrete. Level the concrete by pulling a straight board across it. After the concrete slab has set at least 24 hours, you are ready to begin the barbecue proper. Cinder or concrete block is used as a back filler and is usually laid up first. As you set them, insert metal ties as recommended by your dealer. These ties will hook onto the pieces of stone veneer as you lay them up. Take care in your planning to allow enough room for the stone veneer. Firebrick is used to line the wall and floor of the firebox. This won't crack or split when the fire is red hot. For adhering the veneer to the block, use a mortar mix of one part cement to three parts sand mixed to a workable consistency. Then proceed to lay stones, using plenty of mortar (no voids behind stones).

Individual stones should be laid as they would lie on the ground, not be set on end or in other unnatural positions. Also do not set stones of the same size and shape side by side. Make the joints as thin as possible and fill completely with mortar. After you have laid several stones, smooth out joints before the mortar sets, with a dull-pointed stick. Thoroughly brush off all excess mortar, taking care not to let any cement harden as you go.

Keep the metal grill handy and place into position during construction. Don't wait until the mortar is hard to set it.

Finally, add coping pieces on top to give the barbecue a finished and professional look.

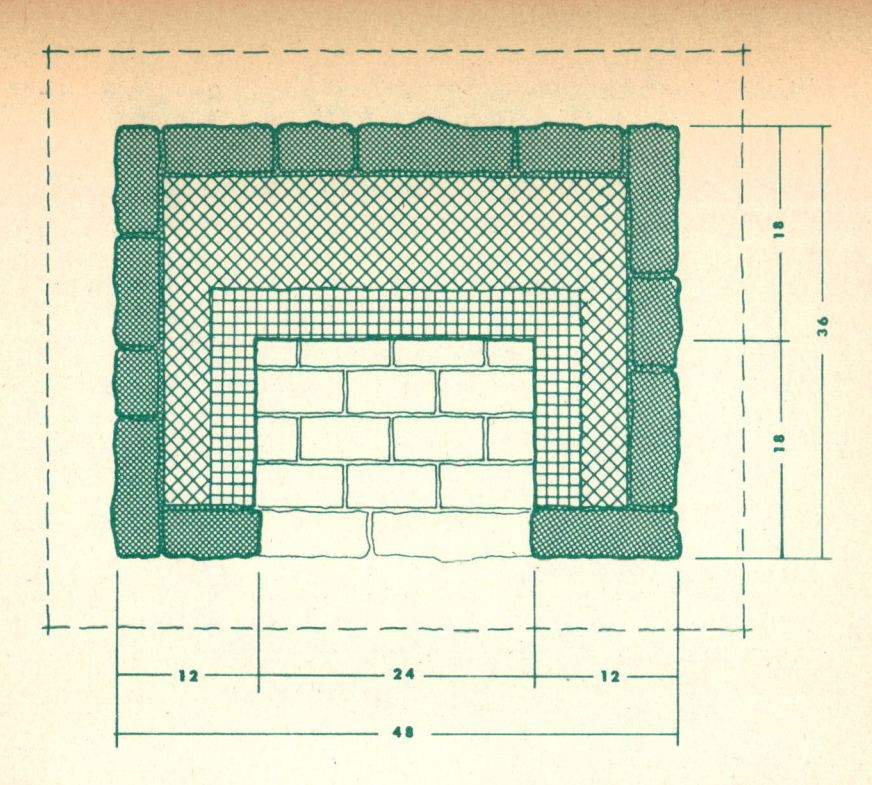

■ STONE
▨ BLOCK
▦ FIREBRICK

Stone barbecue requires a lot more skill than brick one, but can be done. See text.
Building Stone Institute

MATERIALS NEEDED

¾ to 1 ton 4 inch stone veneer
50 firebricks
20 8-inch cinder or concrete blocks
6 4-inch cinder or concrete blocks
1 18-inch x 24-inch grill
3 pieces coping stone
4 bags cement
½ yard of sand
¼ yard of gravel

57

Combination of brick, and stone retaining wall, pretty flowers is attractive, functional.

MISCELLANEOUS PROJECTS

We couldn't find a neat place for these projects, but you surely will.

There are a number of other projects that can add beauty, use, value or just plain fun to outdoor living that are not readily categorized. That's what you'll find in this chapter... everything from a simple brick edging for a lawn or gardening area to how to build a stone retaining wall. Take a look. You're sure to find something that you'll want to get launched on.

A NICE EDGE FOR YOUR LAWN

Brick edging around the lawn is not only good looking (some 10,000 colors and textures of brick you have to choose from), but functional: it makes mowing and trimming chores simpler.

The one shown here is super-simple to do. First, use a flat-bladed spade and dig

Simple brick edging is made by first digging narrow trench for bricks with shovel, then...

Sand base is then laid and the bricks set on top. Joints are then filled with more sand.

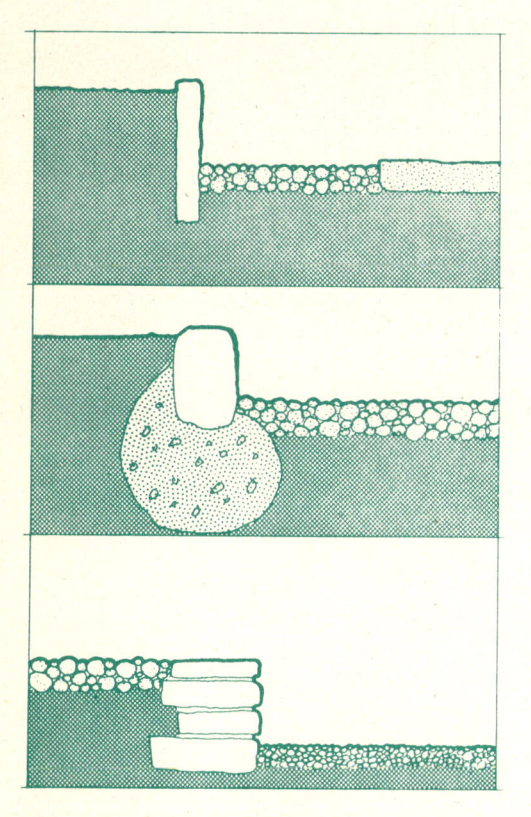

Other decorative edgings, these made with stone. Top, flat stone and gravel; middle, stone in concrete; bottom, mortared flags.

up the sod to a depth of 4-inches and 10-inches wide following the "path" you want the edging to follow.

Lay down about 2-inches of fine sand, then simply lay the brick on the sand with ½-inch joints, tapping each in place with a rubber mallet. Wherever the "path" curves you can fan the bricks slightly; or, cut pieces off to make them fit. When finished, fill all joints with sand.

STONE EDGING

Stone curbing and edging enhances gardens or driveways and acts as a demarcation line between areas. Many types and shapes of stone are available for this purpose. Check with a stone dealer.

There are two basic ways of setting stone curbs or edging: (1) dry in sand or dirt, and (2) in concrete.

The dry way is relatively easy. You place the stone in a slightly excavated trench and pack the dirt around it, keeping the stone level.

The concrete method requires the digging of a larger trench into which a concrete mix of one part cement, two parts sand and four parts gravel is poured. The curb is set in the wet concrete in such a way that no concrete is allowed to show. If you prefer to space the blocks so that there are visible joints between, the joints must be filled with mortar made of one

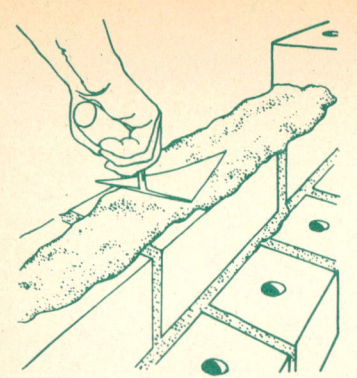

HOW TO LAY BRICK

Use trowel to furrow bed of mortar

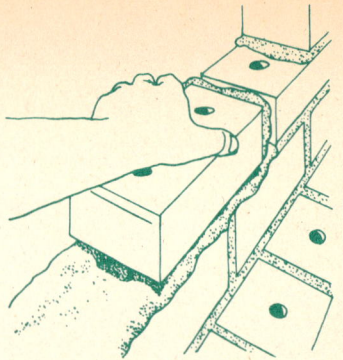

"Butter" the brick and shove in place

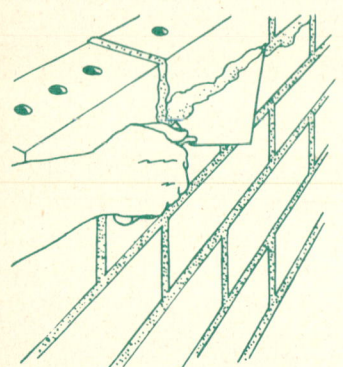

Clip off and reuse excess mortar

Tool joints for best weather resistance

Mailbox is super sturdy brick. Note rod that ties bricks together sticking out at top.

Brick Inst.

Finished mailbox seems to extend out in thin air, but it is actually well supported.

part cement and three parts sand mixed to a workable consistency with water.

A layer type of curb is really a small retaining wall in which small flat stones are placed one upon another. Generally speaking, the gravity of one on another holds the curb in place. However, these, too, can be set in a mortar mix.

Keep in mind that all types of curb can be set in either dry dirt or wet concrete mix.

BRICK MAILBOX

This is a somewhat complex building project, but results in a solid, handsome mailbox that will last as long as the house.

The components of the box are heavy: the posts each weigh in at 130 pounds. So, do work near the site you select. And work on level ground, or off a plywood panel. The site itself should be on earth that has not been disturbed. If it's not compact, the mailbox can ultimately sink a bit and go out of plumb.

The mailbox is built upside-down, then turned over and set in place. The excavation should be deep enough so the base goes below frost level; it's best to check with your local building code department to find out their regulations.

Use hollow core bricks (you'll need 60 or so) and ¼-inch pencil rod reinforcing wire, cut to the following lengths: 2, 4-inches each; 2, 6-inches each; and 4, 8-inches each. These are threaded through holes in the mortar-filled bricks for support. You'll also need two lengths of ½-inch reinforcing bar, each 53-inches long. These are run through the entire structure, including the base.

The posts are identical. Start making each by placing three bricks end-to-end, mortared together. (See sketch). If you wish, you can make a miniform of wood strips to set the bricks in. Fill the designated core with mortar and insert a 4-inch bar in it. Cut and place two full bricks and a half brick in place on top of the first three (threading through holes); fill designated cores with mortar and insert one 6-inch and two 8-inch lengths. Finally, cut and place a half and a full brick over the others, filling the cores with mortar. Also, as you are placing each series of bricks, apply a normal amount of mortar between courses.

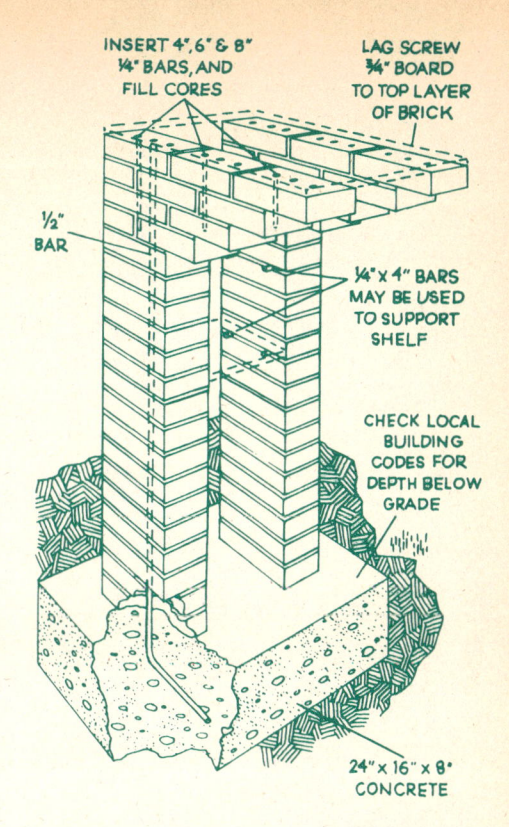

Now, stick the length of ½-inch rod into the designated holes and, applying mortar as you go, thread individual bricks over the rod to build up the height of the post as shown in the drawing. Take care to fill cores completely.

When all bricks are in place, brace your brickwork securely on all four sides until the mortar sets (about a week). Cover to protect against weather.

Next, turn the posts over right-side-up and set them side by side in the excavation you've made. Before doing so, however, bend over the bars sticking out of the bottom so they don't stick into the excavation. Use a short piece of pipe for this (just slip it over the end of the bar) or a wrench.

Support the posts in the hole by bracing each with lumber on all four sides; keep them the proper distance apart by wedging a 2x4 between them.

Use a level to establish that they're plumb. When they are, pour the concrete into the hole. Allow to set for two weeks, covering the top of the posts to protect them.

DRY RETAINING WALL

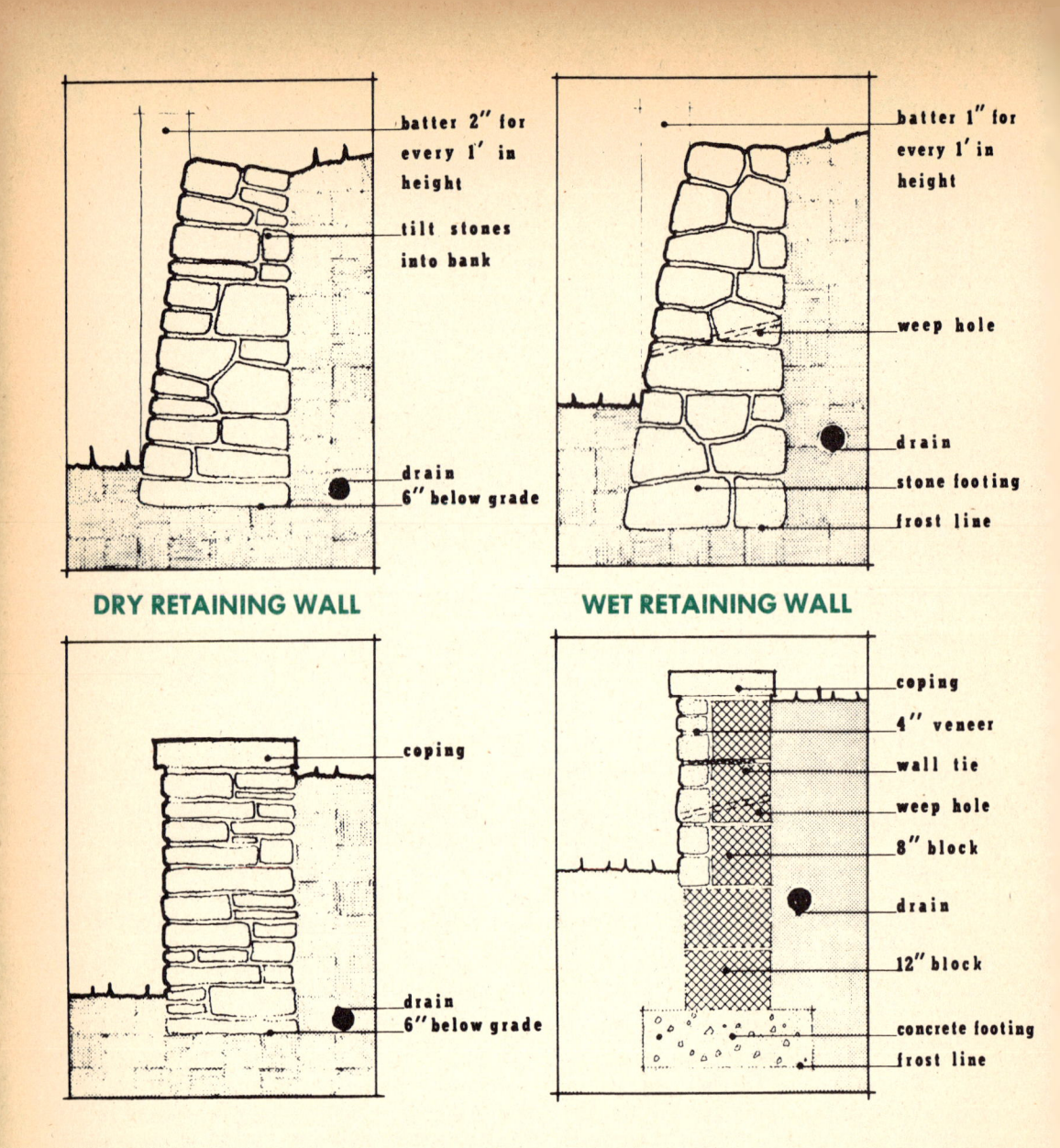

- batter 2" for every 1' in height
- tilt stones into bank
- drain 6" below grade

WET RETAINING WALL

- batter 1" for every 1' in height
- weep hole
- drain
- stone footing
- frost line

- coping
- drain 6" below grade

- coping
- 4" veneer
- wall tie
- weep hole
- 8" block
- drain
- 12" block
- concrete footing
- frost line

To attach the mailbox, first drive wooden plugs into the open cores of the top bricks. Then cut a plank to cover the brickwork neatly and attach it to the top by driving lag screws into the plugs. For good looks, it's best to cut the plank to the size of the bottom of the mailbox you pick. Attach redwood firring strips to the plank so the mailbox fits over them and you can nail the flange on the mailbox to the planks.

DRY RETAINING WALL

A dry retaining wall is constructed without mortar. It is attractive and relatively simple to make. It depends upon the weight and friction of one stone on another for stability. Therefore, walls over 2-feet high require a "batter" (more about this in a moment) of 2-inches back for every 1-foot in height.

SWING

When starting a dry wall, lay the first stones about 6-inches below grade. (No elaborate footing is required for a dry wall since the stones are not bonded together and will raise and lower with the frost). The first stone layer, or "course," should be larger stones. String a line along the wall as a guide to keep it straight.

Batter boards are wedge shaped, flat on one side, sloping on the other. When driven into the ground at the edge of the wall, they afford a quick check on inward sloping. Be certain the batter board is at right angles with the ground by checking with a level.

For best results, lay stones as they would

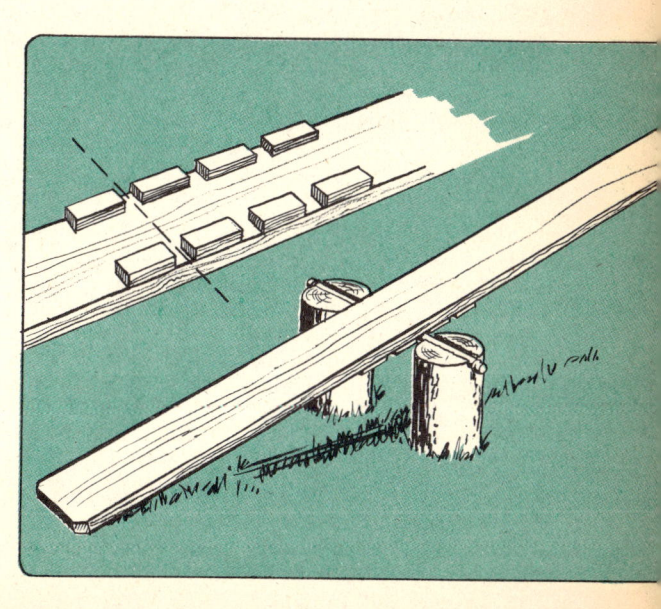

TEETER TOTTER

63

lie naturally on the ground. Don't turn them on end. As you lay them, pack the back of the stones with earth, tying some stones into the earth by using larger pieces. Try to break up joint lines. A continuous joint is not as attractive, nor as structurally sound. As shown in the drawing, install a continuous drain surrounded by coarse gravel.

If the wall is not to be high (up to 2-feet) a batter is not always necessary because it's not retaining much earth. A stone coping can be placed on this wall as well as on a larger battered wall as an alternative way of finishing the top.

Granite, limestone, marble, sandstone, slate and quartzite are available in many colors and textures for this project.

WET RETAINING WALL

A wet retaining wall is like a dry wall except for one major difference: wall stability is not dependent upon the friction of stone upon stone, but rather on the mortar that bonds the wall. Two requirements of this type of construction are (1) a footing of either solid stone or concrete is required down to the frost line and (2) drainage weep holes must be placed in the wall to allow water to flow out. Major advantage of a wet wall is its solidity. Stones can't get kicked out of place and dirt will not run through as it might in dry wall construction.

After footing is in, construction proceeds almost like a dry wall. The batter on this wall should be 1-inch back for every 1-foot in height. In mixing the mortar, use one part cement for every two parts of sand and mix with water to a workable consistency. Pack all voids solid with mortar to achieve a tight wall, taking care not to get cement on the face of the stones.

Another wet wall variation is one of stone veneer. Pour a concrete footing 8-inches thick by 24-inches wide (for a 12-inch thick wall) at the frost line. Then, lay up concrete or cinder block to just below grade. Lay a 4-inch block, leaving a 4-inch shelf to receive the veneer. Wall ties are placed inbetween the block as it is laid to bond the veneer to the block. This type of construction almost always requires a stone coping of some sort to cover the veneer and exposed block wall. One advantage in this is the unlimited choice of 4-inch veneer stones. In both cases, however, drain tiles should be placed in coarse gravel at the back of the wall, and weep holes (rust-free pipe) must be used throughout the wall to let out water that would accumulate behind the wall.

BACKYARD SWING

In spite of the fact that it is made of wood instead of the steel tubing used in commercial swings, this do-it-yourself version can be as strong or stronger—and a lot less costly. Use good clear lumber, redwood or cedar 4x4's if your lumberyard has them; otherwise, use fir or other wood, first treating it with a preservative.

Construction throughout is with 3/8 x 8-inch lag screws, except for the two eye bolts at the top, which hold the braces and provide a place to tie the swing ropes. Shop for chromium-plated screws and screw-eyes, and you'll spare yourself the problem of early rusting.

As the drawings indicate, the swing is made of a pair of A's with a vertical post coming out of the peaks. The length of this post determines the height of the swing; 10-feet is about right for the average youngster, and the drawings are based on that height.

You'll find that the job goes fast if you use a chainsaw efficiently. For instance, a 30 degree cut in the center of a 16-foot, 4x4 provides the angled ends of a pair of the long diagonals of the A's. Stack two or more pieces of 4x4 on a sawbuck, and you can cut them in one pass, saving time and producing accuracy.

Pick a flat area like the garage floor and lay out the first of the A-units. Drill through the member that the lag screw goes through with a 3/8-inch bit, then use a 1/4-inch bit to drill into the member that the screw goes into. This insures a perfectly strong joint. Drive the screws, using a washer in each case.

Construct the second A-unit right on top of the first. This is a time-saver—and it insures accuracy in making the A's identical.

Stand the units up on edge—that is, with one leg and the top on the ground—

WHIRLIGIG

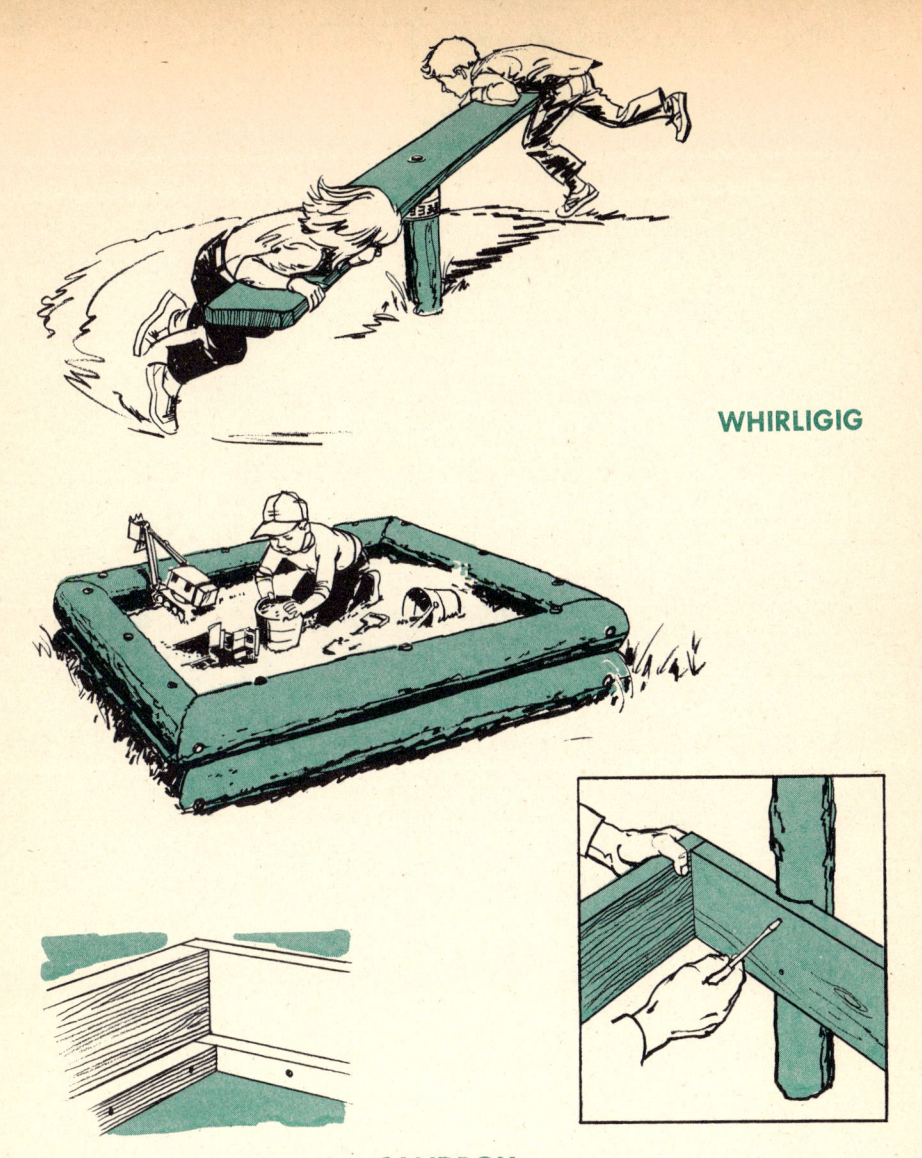

SANDBOX

and place the cross member and diagonals in approximate position while you mark the locations where the holes must be drilled. Then drill the holes. (NOTE: The eye-bolts will require ¼-inch holes through both members.)

Take the components out in the yard, where you'll erect the swing, and stand them up—perhaps leaning one against your step ladder—perhaps enlisting the help of a neighbor. Fasten the cross member in place, then run the screws that hold the lower ends of the diagonals.

Finally, insert the eye bolts and tighten the nuts that hold them in place. See illustrations for final detail of all joints. All that's left is to tie the rope's ends to the eye bolts, then cut those good old-fashioned notches in the end of the board you use for a seat.

HINT: You can make a swing seat that can't get lost, by mounting an eye bolt at either end of the board, tying the lower ends of the rope to these eyes.

THREE BACKYARD FUN-MAKERS

Generations of kids have enjoyed these three backyard fixtures—and yours will too. They're easy to make, using a chain saw.

A TEETER-TOTTER

For the teeter-totter, or see-saw, sink two posts, each about 5-inches in diameter, about 12-inches apart so they stick up about 24-inches. An easy way to do this is to dig a hole big enough to accept both posts . . . set them in place . . . then fill in around them with dirt, tamping it firmly as you fill.

With the posts in place, cut a groove in the top of each post, as shown. These grooves will accept a length of 1-inch galvanized pipe, long enough to span the two posts. Screw regular pipe caps on the ends of the pipe.

For the rocker, pick out a good, sound 2x12 at the lumberyard. About 12 or 14-feet is long enough. Nail some 1x2 cleats to the bottom of the 2x12, as shown in the sketch. These keep the plank from sliding on the pipe, and lets the kids adjust it when one of them is heavier than the other.

A WHIRLIGIG

The whirligig takes just one post. Set it the same way as for the teeter-totter or, for extra rigidity, use concrete. Again, use a good 2x12, 12 or 14-feet long, but in this case it mounts on the post with a single ½-inch lag screw about 6-inches long—with a big washer. The screw goes through the exact middle of the plank and into the exact center of the post. A good idea: invert a 2 pound coffee can over the post, to cut down friction and wear. If the post is bigger, use a gallon paint can.

A SANDBOX

The sandbox, as the pictures show, is nothing more than two rectangles of logs, identical in size, one atop the other. The size is up to you.

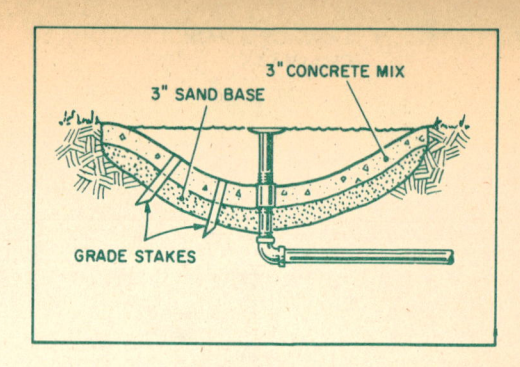

FREE-FORM POOL

SAWHORSE

First, cut the logs to length, then miter the ends. Spike the two rectangles together. Put one on top of the other and spike it in place. Fill with sand to just below where the two rectangles join.

FREE-FORM CONCRETE POOL

A free-formed pool is one which requires no wood form and no construction planning beyond determining the shape, size and depth. For ease in construction, dig so that the pool is shaped like a saucer, rising gently at the sides. A good finished depth for fish is 14-inches. For plant growth, 16 to 18-inches would be better.

1. For a pool 14-inches deep, excavate to a depth of 20-inches. Outside dimensions should be 12-inches greater than the finished dimensions of pool—6-inches on each side. This allows for a 3-inch stone or sand base and 3-inch thickness of concrete.

2. For overflow pipe, use a 2-inch pipe as shown and run to drain, or to a dry well

SAWHORSE FOR A CHAIN SAW

A chain saw is engineered for two-hand operation, so, for easier use, you need a means of holding the stock firmly in place while you cut it. The answer: a sawbuck—which has been the sawyer's helper since pioneer days.

Make yours of light logs—about 4-inches in diameter—or of 2-inch lumber, whichever is handier for you. Construction is simple.

1. Chainsaw four lengths of log or 2x6, 3-feet long, and two that are 2-feet long.

2. Assemble the four 3-foot pieces into a pair of X's, leaving about a foot above the cross points. Long spikes or lag screws will give you a strong joint.

3. Adjust the two X's to exactly 90 degrees, then fasten the 2-foot pieces to the legs of the X's, as shown in the drawings. These pieces not only hold the X's together, but also keep them from collapsing.

There is a version of the sawbuck you'll find handy when you are cutting long logs into short lengths. It's a single X fastened together with a ½-inch bolt and a wingnut, so you can fold it into a convenient size for carrying or storage—and open it up for use. Chainsawing is easy when you lift one end of the stock and put the X under it. As you make successive cuts, keep lifting the end of the stock and moving the X back.

constructed of stone. Install coupling as illustrated for easy removal for draining.

3. Drive grade stakes, 9-inches long, 18-inches apart, marked at 3-inches and 6-inches from top of stakes.

4. Put in stone or sand up to the 3-inch mark as shown.

5. Reinforce bottom with ¼-inch bars, 6-inches apart. Bend to the shape of the pool.

6. Mix concrete mix with 1 pint less water per sack than directed, to prevent flowing on slope before setting. Place mix in bottom of pool first and work up sides. Level mix to top of stakes and remove stakes as you go. (These stakes help you obtain a uniform 3-inch thickness of concrete mix.)

7. Finish with wood float or trowel.

8. Then drain and refill with clean water several times before putting in fish.

WORKING WITH BRICK

A number of projects in this book require bricklaying. Following are some tips and hints on materials you'll need and how to do the job.

• For most projects, a bricklayer's (mason's) trowel, mason's string, mason's hand level, rubber mallet, framing square and broad-bladed brick chisel are the basic things you need. A short length of ¾-inch pipe may be used for smoothing mortar joints; you can also make your own tamper (compacter) with a few stout boards: just nail a 2x2 handle to a 1-foot length of 2x6 or 2x8; for a screed—smoother—you can use a straight (and it must be straight) 8-foot long 2x4 with notches at the end so it can ride edging or form boards and smooth out sand at the proper level. A construction-type wheelbarrow (not a gardening type) is also handy.

• Before laying bricks with mortar, lay them out (5 or 6 at a time) dry so you can anticipate problems.

• Some types of brick should be laid dry; others should be dampened first. Ask your dealer about this, based on the project you're doing.

• Mix only a small amount of mortar at a time—as much as you'd use in an hour or two. If it starts to stiffen, add a small amount of water. Consistency should be about that of soft mud. For big amounts of mortar you can rent a power mixer.

• The joints—bed of mortar between bricks—are usually about ⅜-inch.

• To lay brick, make what bricklayers call a "shoved" joint. Spread a bed of mortar to a little more than the prescribed thickness (slightly higher than guide line) then roughen the surface by making a shallow furrow in it with the trowel (you can do three bricks at a time). "Butter" the end of the brick (pack a good glob of mortar on it) then shove it into the mortar bed with a downward movement until its top is level with the string. When you can do this without moving the brick once it is placed, you will be doing professional work.

• After the mortar is "thumbprint" hard, smooth off the joints with a jointer or a piece of pipe, first going horizontally, then vertically to make hard, dense, concave joints.

• To cut brick, first score it on opposite sides by tapping with broad-bladed cold chisel. Then, with the blade pointing inward on one of the score marks, give the chisel a sharp rap with the hammer. A clean break should occur.

67

OUTDOOR STORAGE

Whatever you have outdoors, here are a variety of places to store it.

As in the inside of the house, storage space is required for outdoor living, whether to store items used in working around the property or for just enjoying the patio. Such things as lawn and garden equipment, barbecue supplies, tools, toys and a host of other things all can have a place outside, not only making them easy for you to get at (you don't have to go back inside the house for everything), but storing them outside frees inside space. Indeed, if everyone had proper outdoor space it would even be possible to get the car inside the garage!

Following are a variety of storage projects, each designed to make life easier out of doors.

LEAN-TO SHED

A good place for lawnmowers, rakes, shovels, hoses, and all the rest of the things you use around the yard and garden is this lean-to shed. You can build the one shown here in a weekend, using your chainsaw (project was designed by Homelite chainsaw people). Stack identical pieces and cut them in multiples—a big time saver.

The dimensions of the shed shown are based on the most efficient use of framing lumber and plywood sheathing—but you can modify the size and shape to suit your needs.

Hanging storage cabinet holds all kinds of outdoor things. See text for details on building it.

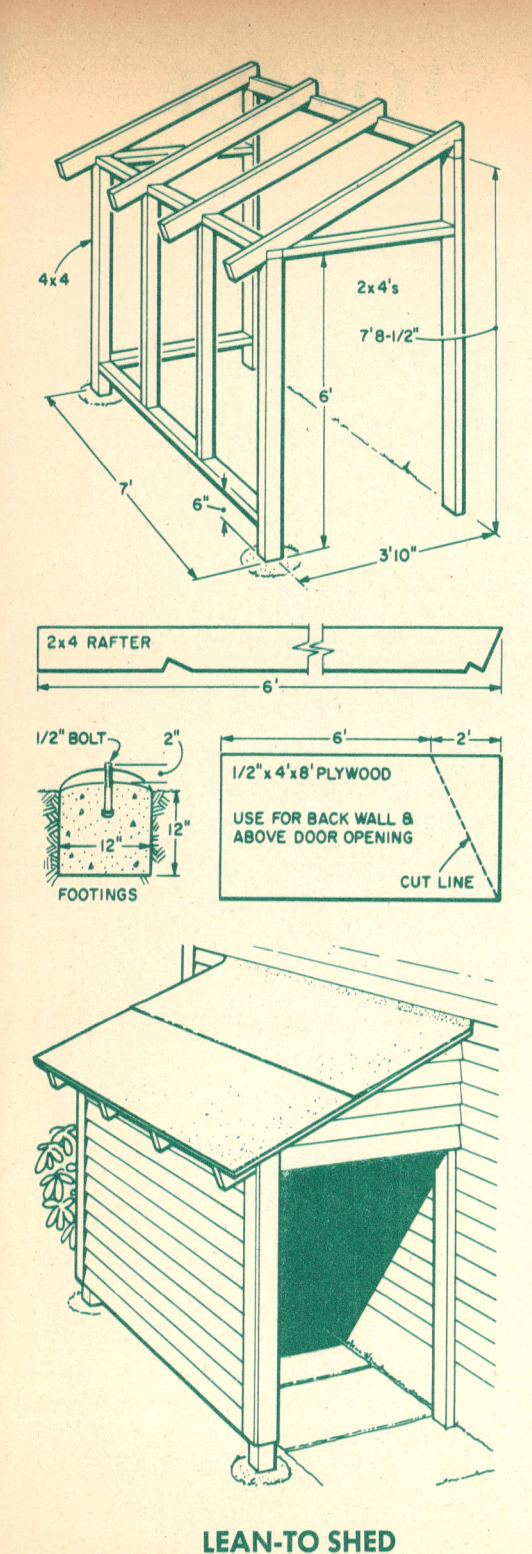

The shed is supported against the building and at the two corners only. Your first step is to provide footings for those corners. Measure out 3'10" from the wall where you'll build, and dig two holes 7-feet apart. Make them about a foot in diameter, about a foot deep, using the 3'10" mark as their center. Fill the holes with concrete, then set a ½-inch bolt, 6-inches long, head down in the concrete, sticking up about 2-inches (see sketch). The bolts should then be exactly 3'10" from the house wall. Let the concrete harden at least three days before you continue construction.

CARPENTRY

Start the carpentry by cutting two 2x4's exactly 7-feet 8½-inches long and nailing them to the wall, exactly opposite the bolts set in concrete. Spike a 7-foot 2x4 across the tops of those on the wall.

Build the outer wall by chainsawing two 4x4's 6-feet long. Working on any convenient flat surface, spike a 7-foot 2x4 across the tops of the 4x4's. Cut-to-fit another 2x4 to go between the 4x4's and toenail it in place 6-inches up from the lower ends. Now cut-to-fit the two studs (verticals).

Now you are ready to cut the four rafters, 6-feet long. The sketch shows how they are angle-cut, and notched near the other end, to fit over the side wall. Toenail the rafters at the top, and into the top of the outside wall. Be certain they are evenly spaced, and parallel, to make it easy to apply the roof.

HOW TO CUT THE SHEATHING

This shed calls for four sheets of ½-inch sheathing-grade plywood. Have your lumber dealer cut them for you into the following sheet sizes:

1   4x8 (this is standard)
1   2x8—this pairs up with the 4x8 sheet to sheath the roof
1   4x7—this is the lower part of the outside wall
1   2x7—this pairs with the above sheet to form the outside wall
1   4x8, cut at an angle, as shown in the sketch. The large piece forms the

HANGING CABINET

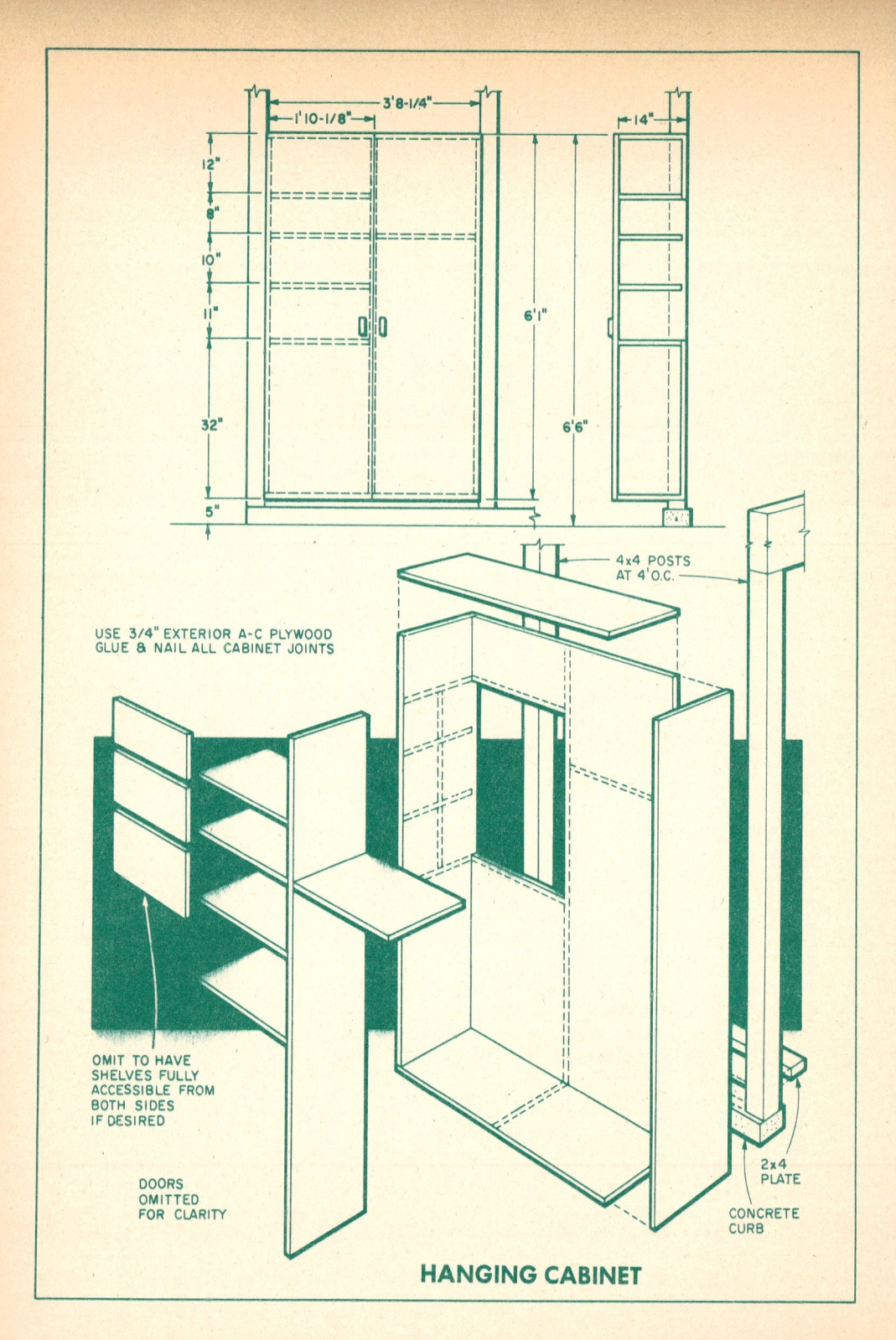

back wall. The small piece goes over the door opening.

With sheathing in place, you are ready to make the shed match the rest of the house . . . simply by applying beveled siding, shingles, or whatever the main house happens to be covered with. If it is some type of masonry, beveled siding would be a good choice.

Use roll roofing on the roof, lapping it up the wall a couple of inches. Nail every 3-inches into the wall. Then use trowel-grade roofing cement to butter a seal along the edge.

NOTE: If you are building the shed against a masonry building, fasten the 2x4's with special masonry nails. And, when you put the roofing on, trowel a bead of roofing cement in back of the edge that laps up the wall, then apply cement all along the joint.

HANGING STORAGE CABINET

This storage unit is simply a relatively shallow box crosshatched inside with shelves. Here it is shown mounted on a carport, but it could really go wherever space is available.

You can make the unit so it's accessible from the back—a good convenience feature in a carport—or make it solid. If you don't want it accessible from both sides, omit shelf dividers indicated. Make back panel solid. The shelves themselves, of course, can be arranged any way that suits your storage needs. It's best, in this regard, to measure the items you'll store in the cabinet before building.

BUILDING THE CABINET

The cabinet is made with A-C exterior plywood. Build it on the floor, completely, as you would any cabinet, making the basic box first, then "filling" it with shelves and hanging doors. Finish it, then hang it on the structure with lag screws or other strong fasteners, penetrating framing members for strength.

FREE-STANDING SHED

A large, free-standing storage shed such as the one shown here will have the bigness to handle just about anything you care to put in it. Even the door works, being equipped with shelves to hold small items. It's 8-feet wide and 6-feet deep, and about 7-feet high.

As with other outdoor projects using plywood, an exterior grade is a must. Material that is $3/8$-inch thick will provide good strength.

Start construction by cutting 2x4-inch floor framing members so that the floor, when assembled, will measure exactly 6x8-feet in width and length, outside to outside. Use 16d common nails and assemble on any reasonably level surface. Set 4x4-inch treated skids in place and check to see that they are level. Toenail floor framing to skids through floor joists. Cut plywood floor panels to size and nail to all supports with 8d galvanized box nails 12-inches off center.

Cut 2x2-inch wall studs and top and bottom plates to length. Lay wall studs out on a level surface at spacings shown and fasten bottom and top plate into place. Lift walls into place and fasten with 8d nails through bottom plate into outside floor framing under plywood. Check with level to be certain framing is plumb. Then, nail through studs to fasten framing at each corner.

Next, apply your choice of plywood sidings such as Texture 1-11, rough-sawn 303 siding or Medium Density plywood with 1x2-inch battens. Fasten with 6d cement-coated or galvanized nails, 6-inch centers around all panel edges and 12-inch centers at other studs.

Cut 2x2-inch rafters to fit ridge and fascia boards. Notch to fit over plates and toenail with 8d nails into plate and ridge board. Cut fascia board to length and nail to ends of rafters. Cut plywood roof sheathing and fasten with 6d common nails to framing at 6-inch centers at panel edges and 12-inch centers elsewhere. Apply 1x2-inch fascia, then install built-up or 90 lb. roll roofing over plywood.

Construct door by fastening cut-to-length 1x6-inch stock lumber with 6d finish nails and glue to plywood siding previously cut to door size. Nail and glue 1x6-inch lumber and $3/8$-inch plywood to 1x6-inch frame on door to form fronts on shelves.

Free-standing shed features doors that work—hard. They hold all little things that can get lost.

Apply 1½ pair of zinc-coated fast-pin hinges and hang door. Install key-lock with hold-open latch. Cut plywood shelves and counter (see detail sketch) to size along with plywood brackets and 2x4-inch supports. Install as shown with 8d common nails or wood screws. Of course, you can make any shelf arrangement inside that suits you. Cut plywood to size for portable ramp to door opening. Assemble after cutting 2x4-inch frame to size.

Finally, use a good quality exterior house paint or stain on your new structure. First, apply a prime undercoat, then two coats of exterior latex or oil base house paint or two coats exterior stain on all plywood and wood surfaces. If you plan a contrasting color for the optional battens, pre-paint or stain them, and when dry, fasten with 6d galvanized box nails.

DOUBLE-DOOR SHED

A sleek variation of the free-standing shed is this one. Resting on a bed of gravel, it features wide double doors which will accommodate the largest piece of outdoor equipment, and an interior that is ideal for attaching hooks, brackets, and shelving, sized to meet your requirements. The redwood or treated-wood sill resists deterioration from ground water, and the roof can withstand a normal snow load. Stained or left to weather naturally, the rough sawn exterior (303 DFPA Rough Sawn Plywood) blends with any outdoor setting.

Occupying 4x8-feet, the unit measures 6-feet 8-inches high in front and 4-feet 6-inches at the rear. It can be permanently attached to the ground with ¾-inch steel-spike stakes bolted to the frame and can

FREE-STANDING SHED

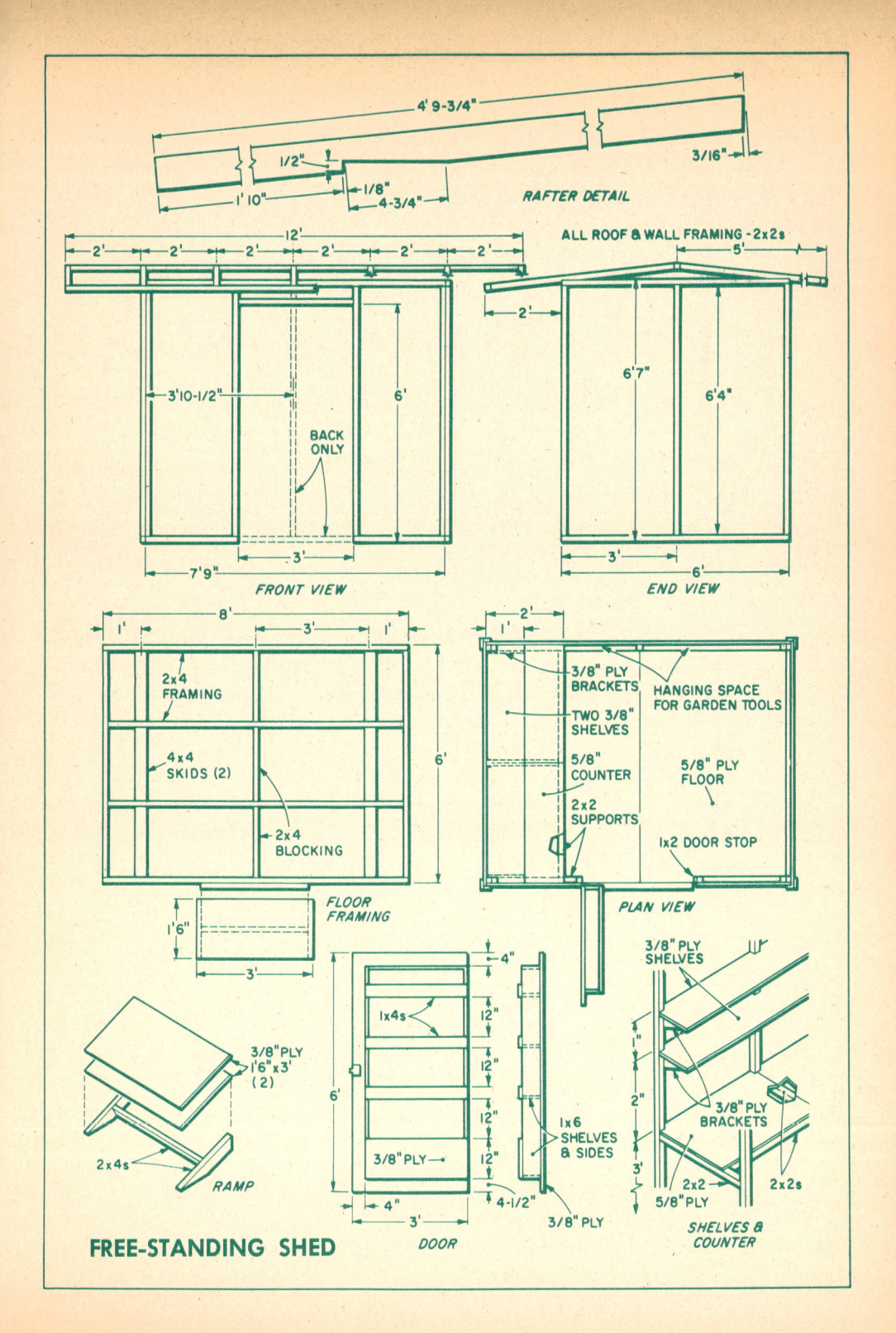

FREE-STANDING SHED

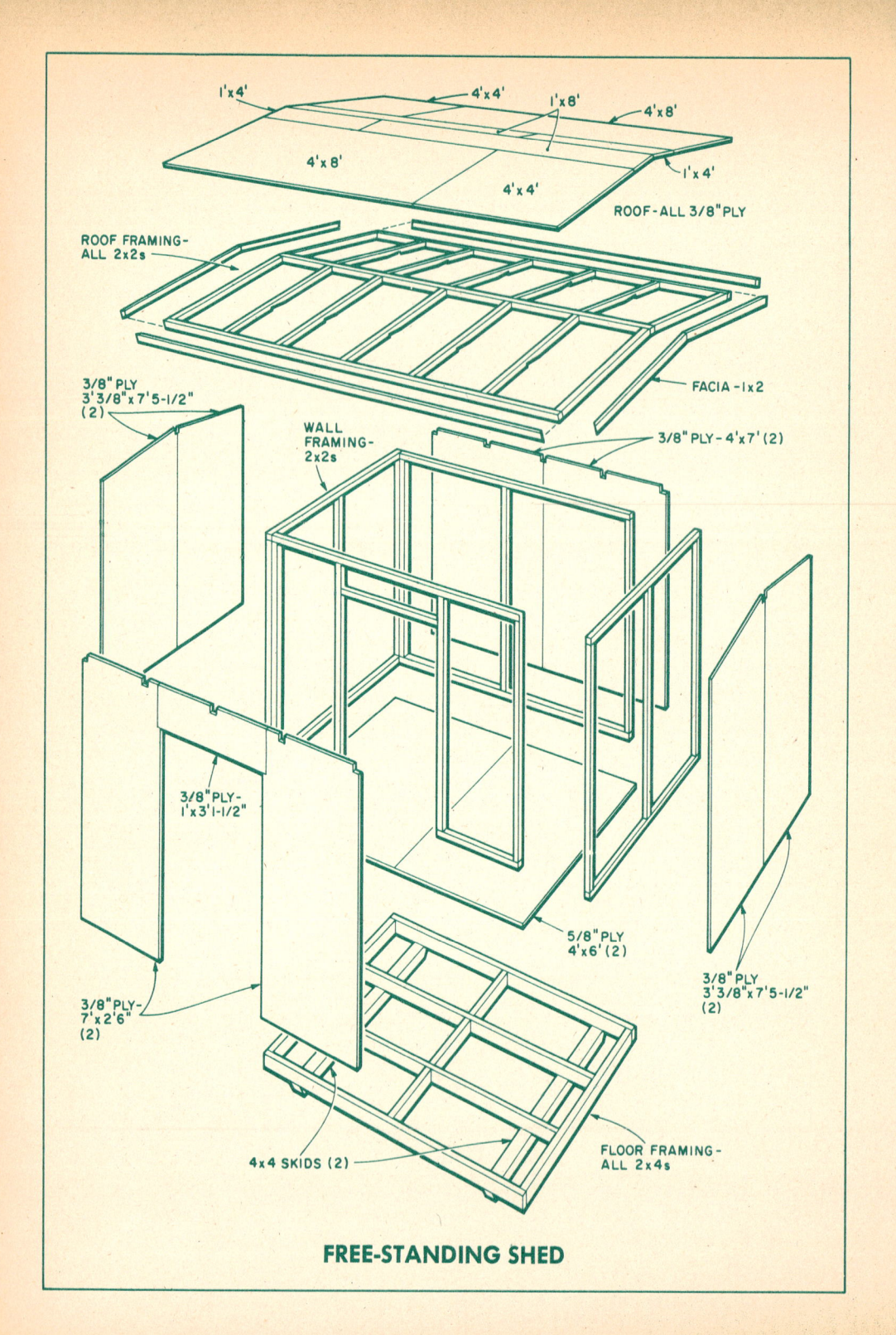

be unbolted and moved to a new location . . . you can take it with you if you move.

Framing is minimal—2x2's for the sides and 2x4's for the roof. The shed is built with a series of panels nailed to framing and fastened together with ⁵⁄₁₆-inch carriage bolts. All hardware is readily available at hardware stores, including hinges and door latch.

A skilled do-it-yourselfer can build this shed over the weekend. A sabre saw and drill will speed and simplify the work.

STORAGE . . . PLUS

When it's outdoor food serving time, the unit shown here can greatly reduce the number of trips the homemaker has to make back and forth between patio and kitchen.

The unit is basically a base cabinet with two large, swing-open doors. It can hold a variety of items, such as the chairs shown. What makes it extra useful, however, is the top. This is simply an upside-

Double-door shed has wide doors to store big things. Note slots for shovels on door.

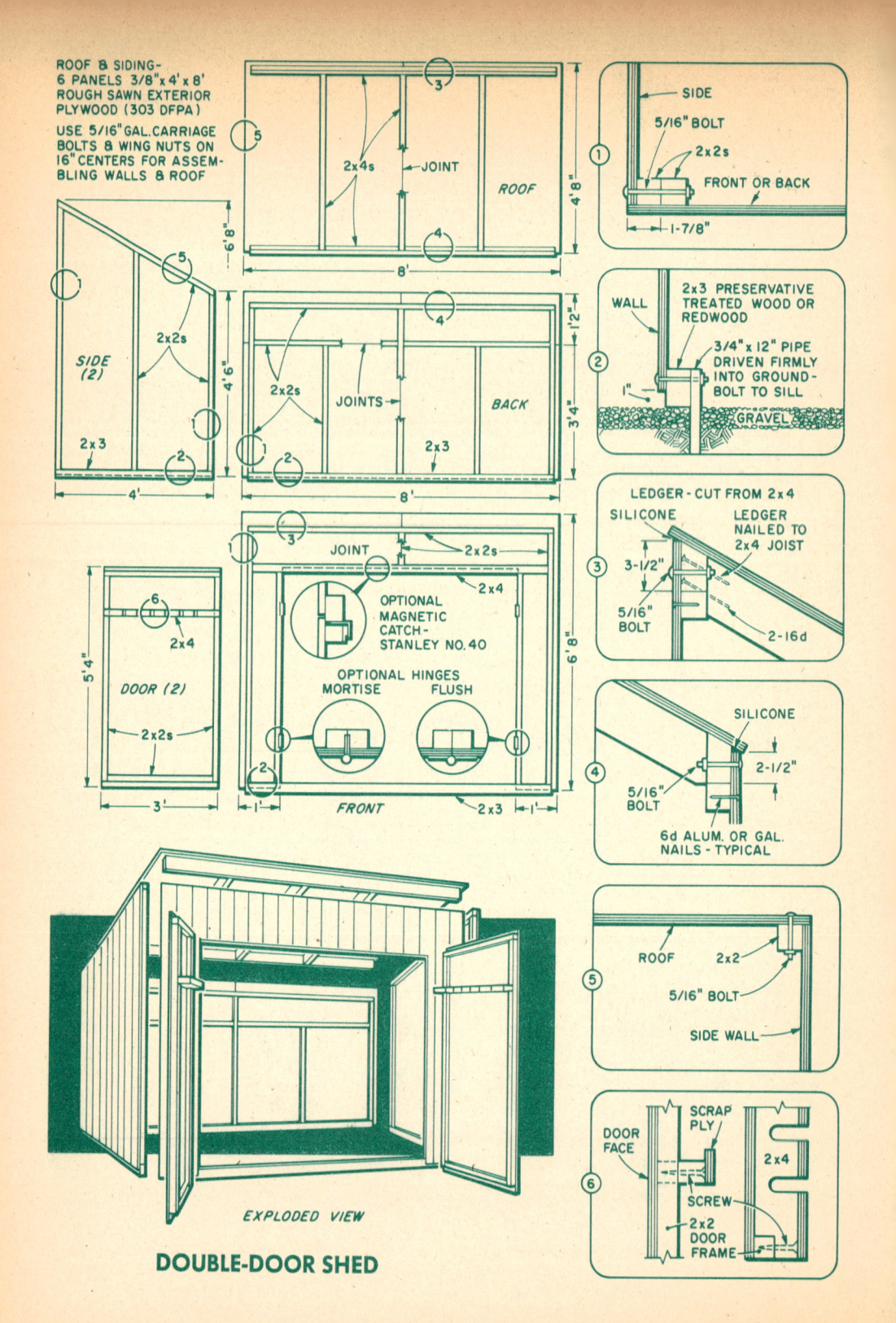

DOUBLE-DOOR SHED

Base cabinet on patio has good storage area for chairs etc., while top functions as server.

down shallow box but it is set right beneath the window. You can open the windows and pass items through onto it; indeed, it can function as a serving counter, or buffet.

Construction is simple. Build a framework of 2x4's and cover it, as is shown here, with tongue and groove redwood boards or other stock that has been treated to stand up to the weather. Use galvanized, stainless steel or aluminum nails.

The top, as mentioned, is simply a shallow box. If you wish, you can have a little extra flair by installing ceramic tile, a colorful seamless flooring material or the like on it. Whatever you choose, make certain that it is resistant to heat.

Chain saw is good tool for outdoor building as well as being "it" for cutting firewood.

77

FENCING FACTS

Fencing makes a pretty way to mark off and frame your property.

A fence can function in a variety of ways. It can give you privacy, corral kids and dogs, keep out—or let in—wind, complement and accent the beauty of your home by providing a "framework" around it.

Before launching into any project however, there are a few things to check out.

First, tell your neighbor(s) what you plan, if the fence will face his property, affect the quality of his life in some way. In some cases—and it's not infrequent—you may be able to team up with a neighbor in building the fence, thereby sharing work and costs. For this, though, you'll have to only consider fences of "good neighbor" design: ones that look good from both sides. If you and your neighbor can't agree on costs or design, you may have to settle for building what you like just inside your property line.

Also, check with local building people. There are likely restrictions on the kind of fence you can build, how high it can be, and where it can be located.

KINDS OF FENCES

There are a variety of fences to select from, each with advantages and disadvantages. Following is a brief roundup.

Brick. Because of cost, and difficulty of building for the average do-it-yourselfer, this kind of fence must usually be kept on a small scale. Built too high, also, it can lend an undesirable "prison" look to a home, unless carefully complemented by shrubbery or plantings.

On the other hand, a low brick fence can be quite attractive and is a good choice when you want to lengthen house lines.

Stone. This shares the disadvantages of

brick, but is even more costly (unless you gather the stones yourself from some free source).

Block. Plain concrete and cinder blocks are usually not considered good-looking enough for fencing. Installation can be accomplished by a determined do-it-yourselfer.

Concrete blocks also come with designs, their faces "sculpted" or worked in some way, with some having voids to allow breezes through. Installation is basically the same as for regular block. They make a very good looking fence, (of any height you wish) but the cost is high.

Chain-Link. This is available both plain and coated with plastic of various colors. Prices vary widely; it's best to compare them very carefully.

For homes, heights of 42-inches or less are usually most attractive. Chain-link requires special stretchers to install and is a job for a professional.

Plastic. This is fencing composed of broad sheets of plastic nailed to wood posts. The plastic is available in a wide variety of colors (including striped), translucent or opaque, textured, "corrugated" and otherwise shaped.

There is no great problem installing posts, and since the plastic is light and easy to cut, doing it yourself is simple. Also, it never needs to be painted or otherwise maintained. Plastic is not expensive, but some people object to it simply because it is plastic (actually, most "plastic" fencing is fiberglass).

Shrubbery. There are a number of living fences you can purchase. Some are designed to grow quite thick and high, affording complete privacy. Among the types available are North Amur River privet, golden privet, boxwood, upright evergreen and honeysuckle. Of course, these fences have to be maintained continually. If you're not the type who likes to tend to a lawn, you won't like these. If you purchase shrubs or hedges as seedlings the cost will be minimal.

Wood. Fences made of wood afford the

Redwood and fiberglass-reinforced fence allows privacy without cutting out all sunlight.
Filon

TYPES OF FENCES

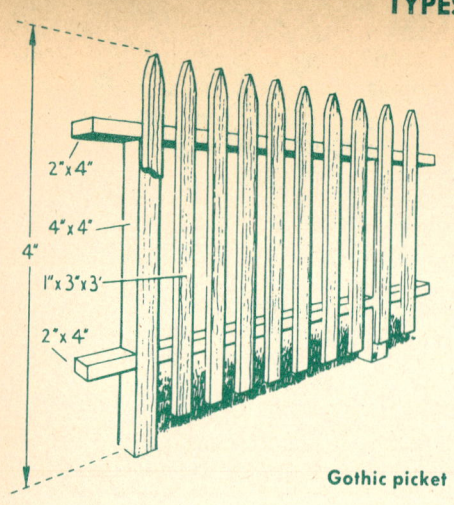

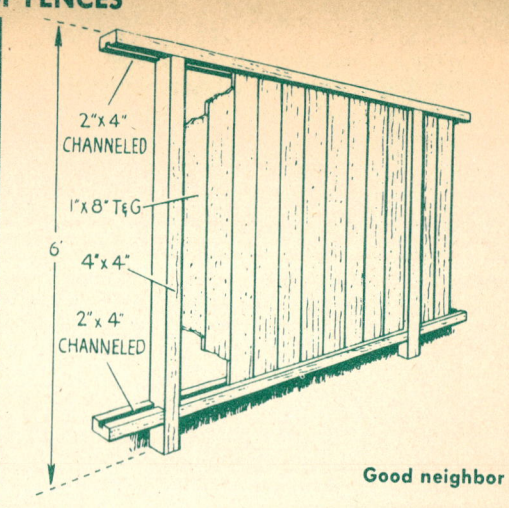

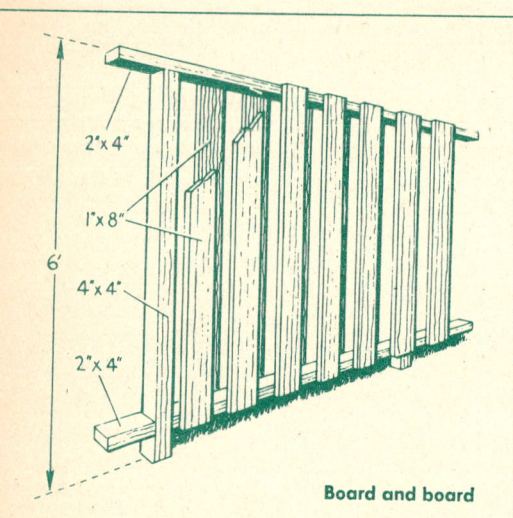

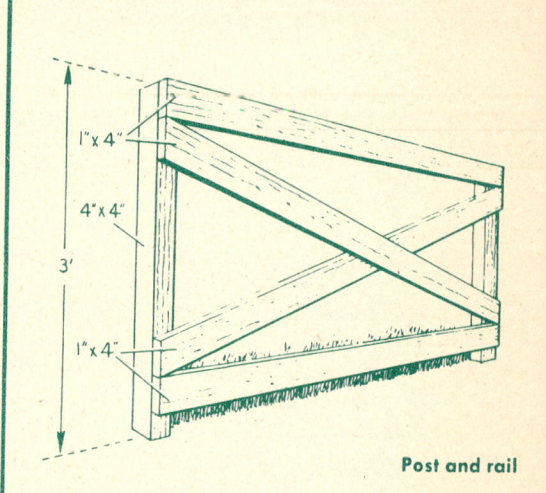

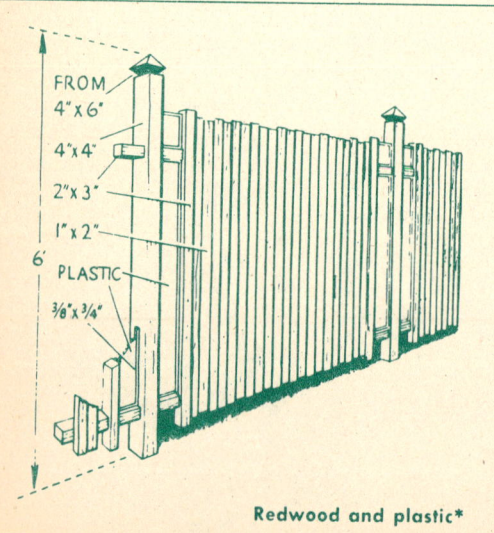

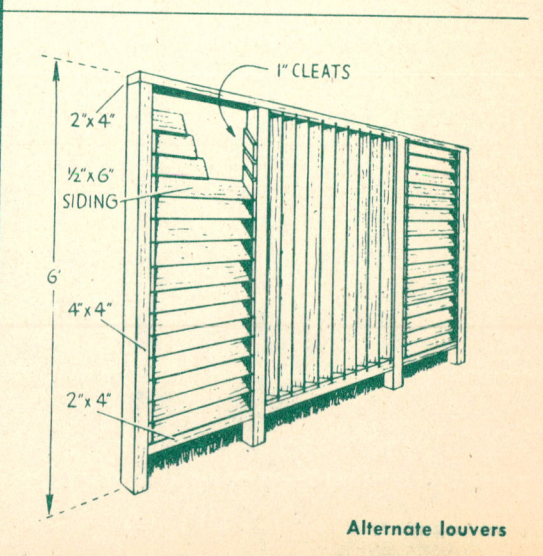

Gothic picket
- 2" x 4"
- 4" x 4"
- 1" x 3" x 3'
- 2" x 4"
- 4'

Good neighbor
- 2" x 4" CHANNELED
- 1" x 8" T&G
- 4" x 4"
- 2" x 4" CHANNELED
- 6'

Board and board
- 2" x 4"
- 1" x 8"
- 4" x 4"
- 2" x 4"
- 6'

Post and rail
- 1" x 4"
- 4" x 4"
- 1" x 4"
- 3'

Redwood and plastic*
- FROM 4" x 6"
- 4" x 4"
- 2" x 3"
- 1" x 2"
- PLASTIC
- 3/8" x 3/4"
- 6'

Alternate louvers
- 1" CLEATS
- 2" x 4"
- 1/2" x 6" SIDING
- 4" x 4"
- 2" x 4"
- 6'

greatest selection. Lumberyards, building supply dealers and other outlets carry it in two basic forms: ready-made sections (usually 8-feet) that you fasten to posts you install, and knockdown—you assemble the fence from scratch with stock pieces.

A number of fence styles are particularly popular.

Board. This is the easiest kind of fence to build. The boards are usually of 1-inch stock and of various widths, either spaced (1-inch or more) or butted. Butting, however, provides a solid front against the

Before installing posts, coat them generously with stain-preservative, especially at ends.

Make sure fence posts are true before anchoring them in concrete or earth. Double check.

FRP material cuts easily with circular saw that is equipped with the proper cutting blade.

Slotted cross braces fit over the pieces of FRP both for good looks and extra strength.

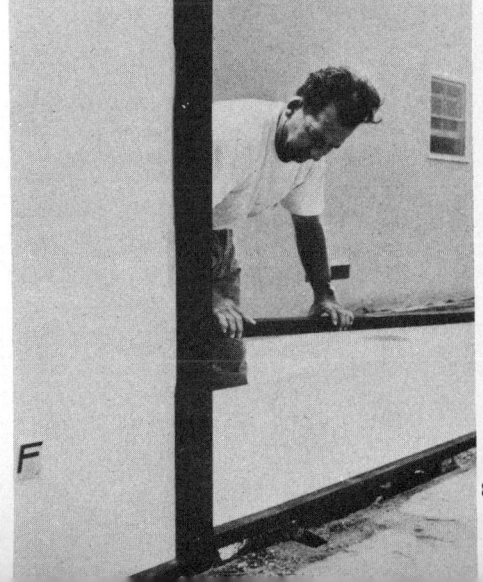

Nail braces to upright posts securely using rust-proof nails. Rust will ruin job quickly.

For neat job, you fit corrugated molding over ends of FRP, then secure them with nails.

wind and may not be desirable in windy areas unless the posts have been most securely anchored.

Board fences can provide any degree of privacy you wish, depending on how far apart the boards are set. One variation on the board fence is the louvered type, with boards set between rails at an angle. This affords a good degree of privacy but lets breezes in.

Basketweave fences consist of flexible boards woven between posts. While affording a solid front—and good privacy—it doesn't look like a billboard; in fact, most people consider it quite handsome.

The *picket* fence is an old standby. Its usual function is simply to dress up or "frame" the property, provide boundary lines.

Pickets are available in a surprisingly wide range of sizes, from 1¼ to 5½-inches wide and 2 to five-feet long; thickness is usually an inch. If you wish, you can also get plastic and metal pickets.

Stockade fence is really for privacy only. It is a solid fence composed of boards that are pointed on top. While it does work well at its assigned task, check carefully with neighbors before installing: they might consider it offensive.

Split rail fences have a rustic charm that is hard to beat. Also, they're inexpensive (if today's wood prices can be termed that) as fences go and simple to make. On the other hand, they don't have any other function than looking good.

INSTALLING A WOOD FENCE

To install a wood fence, start by mark-

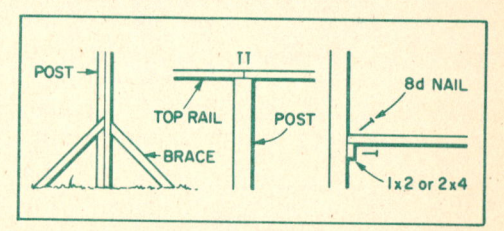

Above left, method of bracing post; middle, nailing rails on; securing rails to posts.

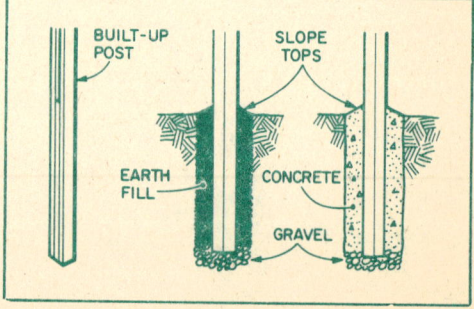

Left, method of building up post; middle and right: two ways to anchor posts in ground.

ILLUSTRATION NO. 3

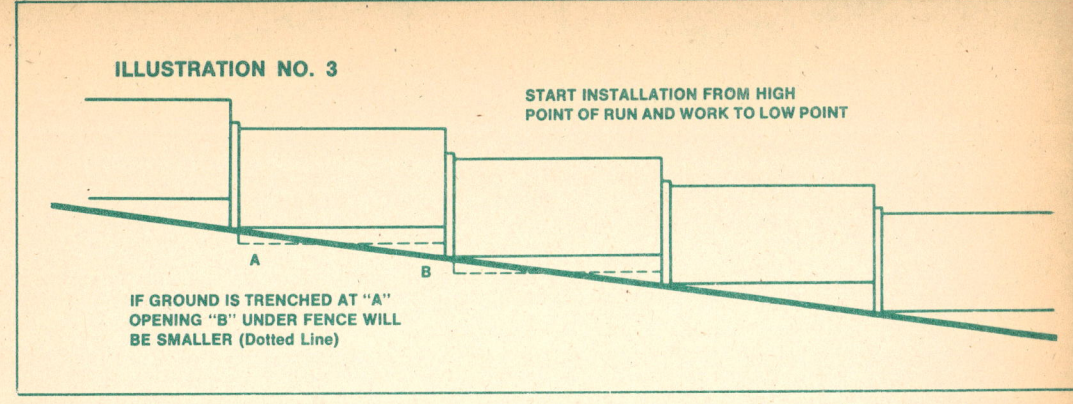

START INSTALLATION FROM HIGH POINT OF RUN AND WORK TO LOW POINT

A B

IF GROUND IS TRENCHED AT "A" OPENING "B" UNDER FENCE WILL BE SMALLER (Dotted Line)

When ground is hilly, set fencing as above. All parts of fence must be true, solidly anchored.

ing off the fence line with a stout line or cord connected to stakes driven into the ground.

All wood fences require that holes be made for the posts. Doing this job with a shovel is very difficult. Much better is a post hole digger, either the clamshell type, if the earth is rocky, or an auger type if the earth is free of large rocks. You can rent manual, as well as electric or gas-powered kinds.

Dig the holes carefully, starting, preferably, at an end post, disturbing as little earth as possible. Each hole should be at least 8-inches in diameter. The easiest way to determine hole depth and spacing between them is to lay out a fence section with the posts in proper relation—just as they'll be when assembled. The part of the post that goes beneath the section is the depth of the hole. The distance between the center of one post and the center of the

Fence here is largely decorative, but it does provide some privacy, keeps stray dogs out.

83

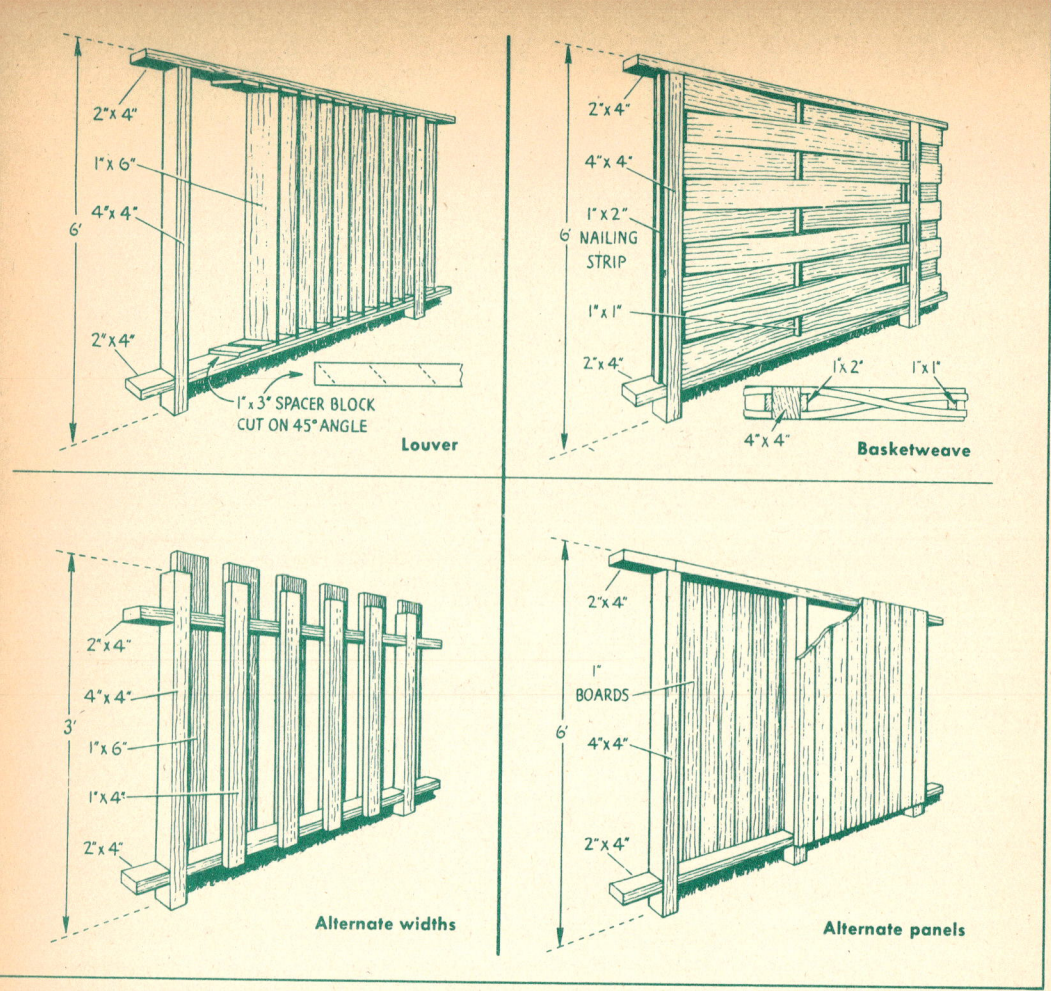

More popular fences. Probably the most popular of those above is the basketweave type.

Most popular gates can be built on simple frames shown in these two illustrations.

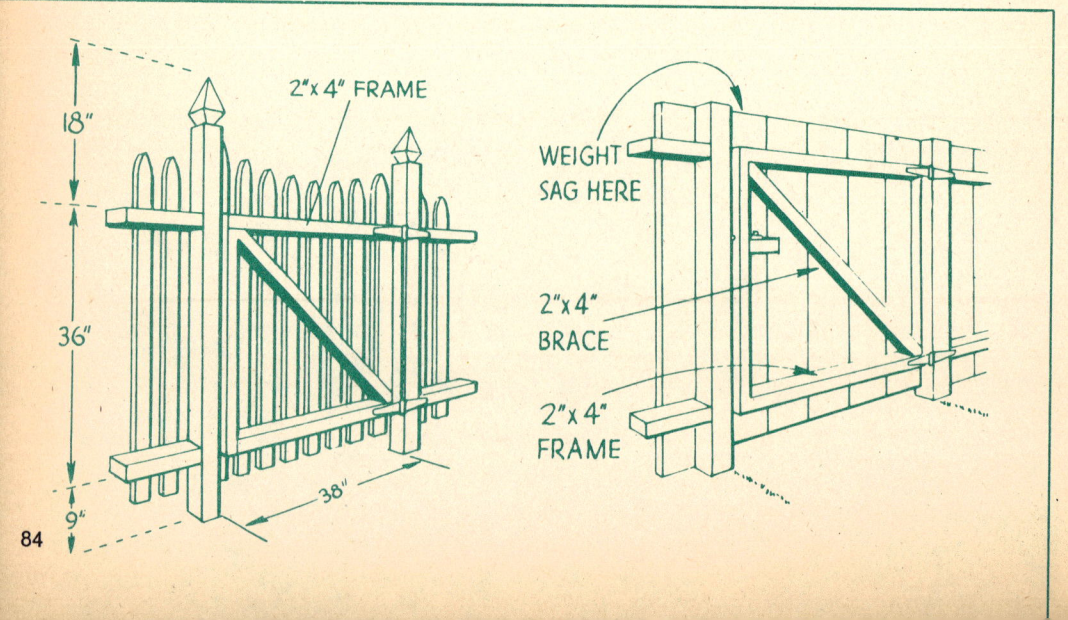

For total privacy, solid board fence of suitable height is the ticket. It keeps kids out too.

next one will give you proper spacing of holes, center to center. On fences with exposed back rails—such as stockade, grapestake and vertical boards—the posts are installed with their tops even with the top back rail. On framed fences without back rails, such as basketweave—posts are installed flush with the fence top, or a few inches above, depending on your preference.

For accuracy, it is better to install wood fence a section at a time, digging the holes as you go.

Posts can be installed in concrete, gravel, or the soil removed from the hole.

After a hole is dug, pack the bottom of it with an inch or two of gravel for drainage. If installing the post with gravel or soil, follow this procedure: Set the post in the hole, then pack around the bottom of it (use a hefty board or commercial tamper) with soil or gravel. Check to see that it is straight and true by laying a level on two adjacent sides. Now, finish packing the hole with soil or gravel, tamping it down firmly as you go. For extra firm packing add a little water to soil—but not so much that it gets soupy.

POSTS IN CONCRETE

If using concrete (not necessary unless the ground is extremely sandy or for some reason a deep enough hole couldn't be dug) follow this procedure: Pack the bottom of the hole with gravel, then set the post in place and tamp several inches of gravel around it. Brace the post straight and true with boards (nail them on). Measure to where the next post will be and repeat the procedure. Install all other posts needed in the particular line of fence, bracing each. Then come back and fill all holes with concrete, slanting it at the top of the hole so water can run off (You should do this with soil or gravel, also). After concrete sets up, remove the braces.

Once the posts are in, it's a simple matter to nail on the fencing proper, using the nails specified (usually galvanized to prevent rust). As you go, you'll find it necessary to trim sections or pieces to fit. Power saws come in handy here, especially with solid fences such as basket-weave.

GATES

At some point in your fence a gate will be required. Rather than set the posts first, it will be easier to attach the gate to the hinge-side post and then set it and the latch side post as a single, independent unit. To do this, lay the gate and its two posts on the ground in their proper "standing up" positions. Attach the gate to the post, then set the latch hardware in the gate and post, following instructions that come with it. Allow ¼-inch to ½-inch clearance on both sides of the gate, and 2 or 3-inches clearance at the bottom; this is especially necessary in areas of snow and ice, which can clog up and make the gate difficult to open.

FINISHING

Your dealer will have specific advice on how to finish your fence, and whether it requires a preservative. In general, for posts—which come in contact with ground—good woods are the heartwood of Cedar, all-heartwood Redwood and any of the western woods—Douglas Fir, Englemann Spruce, Idaho White Pine, Sugar Pine, Western Larch, etc.—that have been pressure-treated with a preservative. If the wood is not in contact with the ground, preservative is not usually necessary.

Wood may be painted, stained or left to weather naturally. If you use redwood or cedar, two of the most popular fencing woods, it hardly makes sense to paint them. The wood has a natural beauty—they weather to a silvery gray color. With redwood, however, you should apply a coat of stain upon installation and every two or three years thereafter. Redwood can turn dark in spots—even black—and the stain will enable it to weather uniformly. Once you paint your fence it means that you're saddling yourself with a permanent maintenance job.

Slim slat fence allows gentle cooling breezes in but from certain angles gives good privacy.

Buster Crabbe Pools

There are few better ways to beat the heat than a pool—and you can build it by yourself.

A COOL WAY TO BEAT THE HEAT

Whether you choose a below or above-ground pool, build it yourself.

A pool can do a lot for you. Besides letting you and your family beat the heat, it can mean that you can avoid traffic tie-ups on the way to the beach, provide the best kind of exercise for everyone and improve the value of your home (though it will also slightly raise taxes).

Before taking the plunge, however, you should know what's available, the advantages and disadvantages of each type. While prices can go much higher—and lower—the average cost of a pool today is around $5000.00. That deserves careful consideration in anyone's language.

IN-GROUND POOLS

There are basically two kinds of pools: in-ground, which refers to ones partially or totally in the ground; and above-ground, where the pool rests on the ground.

The in-ground types are the more expensive and likely to please more members of the family, since they commonly

87

come with a deep, as well as shallow end. Above-ground types are usually 4-feet high.

Two kinds of in-ground pools dominate the market, accounting for over 90% of sales. The first is the sprayed concrete type, also called the Gunite pool. This must be installed by skilled workmen. It basically involves installing a wire mesh in the excavation, then spraying concrete over it, and some type of smoothing material applied over the concrete (concrete itself is abrasive).

As a do-it-yourselfer, you'll likely want to avoid a Gunite pool—it's definitely a job for professionals. Its disadvantages as a pool are that it can crack, especially in cold climates, algae can develop and, like all concrete pools, it has to be painted fairly frequently (anywhere from once a year to up to five years).

On the positive side, this type of pool can last a lifetime, can be installed quickly and, since they're seamless, can be made into any shape you like, from rectangular to kidney. Cost of this type of pool ranges from about $5000 up (the area you live in affects price—the more competitive the better).

Gunite pools account for over 45% of sales. Equally popular, and definitely a do-it-yourself pool, is the vinyl-lined type.

VINYL-LINED POOL

These pools come in kits with all you need to do the job included. Basically, they consist of walls—steel, aluminum or treated wood—and a 20 to 30 gauge vinyl liner which is draped over the walls and into the excavation, which is lined with sand and peat moss.

Advantages of the vinyl-lined pool are: lower cost than most pools—$4000 to $5000; less maintenance—the vinyl liner can stand temperatures of 30 to 40 degrees below zero and algae has difficulty growing on it. The vinyl never needs to be

Above-ground pool is a popular type. One shown is equipped with a good deal of extras.
Coleco Pools

painted and you needn't drain the pool over the winter. Also, it can be installed fast—five days or less.

Disadvantages are that the vinyl can puncture, and it can get to the point where the liner must be replaced. Most tears however can be repaired with an inexpensive patch kit that you can use underwater.

ABOVE-GROUND POOLS

This type of pool consists of walls—steel, aluminum, or treated wood—supports, railing and a vinyl liner. Most of them have a depth of 4-feet, but they are also available with an expandable liner that allows a depth at one end of 7 or 8 feet, making them partially built-in.

The above-ground pool has a number of advantages. First, you don't have to tear up your backyard, as you do with a below-ground type. Second, cost is low—$500 or $600. Third, it's an easy do-it-yourself job. Fourth, in most areas they won't be counted as a home improvement, because you can take them with you if you move.

On the minus side, above-ground pools can only be expected to last around 10 years—they're not as durable as the in-ground types. Second, above-grounders are limited as to shape, usually being oval or round. Finally, if a part needs replacement or repair, it is difficult to get the dealer to visit your home.

Pools come in a variety of sizes usually in multiples of 4-feet. Most range from 15 by 30 feet to 20 by 40 feet. Experts feel that, assuming the pool fully occupied, each swimmer should have 36 square feet and 100 square feet per diver.

There are a huge variety of accessories

Photos from Buster Crabbe Pools

First step in building pool is to mark out area to be excavated with lime, stakes, string.

Backhoe does the digging. It can be rented, but it really is a job for a professional.

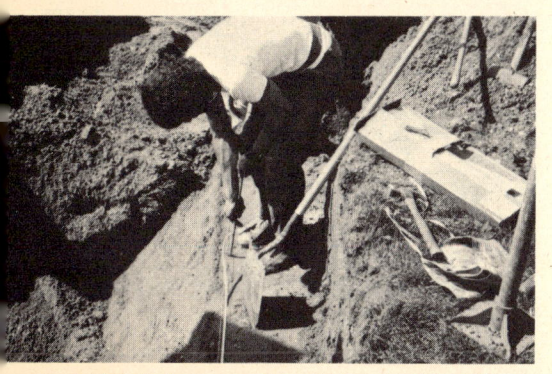

Ledge is dug out of earth. Pool walls will rest on it, be supported securely with braces.

Wall panels are butted together. You can put up a lot of pool in a short period of time.

Panels are joined at corners with steel angle. Power tools are must for installation.

Receptor rails are installed along tops of the panels. Pool coping goes on top of them.

Power saw makes fast work of cutting notch in panel for combination skimmer-feeder.

Filter is first set securely in place, then the edges are covered with a waterproof taping.

Throughout installation, it is important to check for square. Diagonal line does this.

Good supply of sand is poured into graded excavation. Spread smoothly with a rake.

After the sand is graded, it is tamped firmly down and formed by hand with tamper.

Sand is then troweled into smooth shape. In photo worker is doing hopper end of pool.

With sand prepared, vinyl liner is unrolled onto pool. You'll need helpers at this step.

All air is then sucked out beneath liner by means of a vacuum, drawing it good and tight.

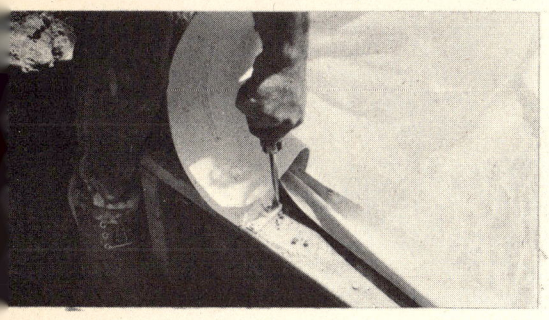

Liner is secured to pool panels and coping is locked into place on top of the liner.

Accessories such as ladder, diving board are installed only after liner is securely in place.

available for pools, including heaters (which can extend pool use a couple of months), slides, underwater lights, winterizing covers, vacuum cleaners, hand leaf skimmers, automatic cleaning systems, and many other things. All these, of course, add to the cost—but you don't have to install them all at once.

INSTALLING A VINYL-LINED POOL

As mentioned, this is not a difficult job for the do-it-yourselfer.

The first thing to do in installing the pool is to outline the pool perimeter with lime. Make sure that you won't be digging down into sewer lines or other cables. Also,

91

If you like, you can get a pool with all plywood walls. They are very strong, durable.

if possible, avoid being too near trees—the leaves and seeds can cause cleaning difficulties. And, of course, the pool should be in a sunny location.

The next part of the job—excavation—must be done professionally by someone with a backhoe. Expect to layout $100 to $150 for this. Plans provided with the pool will show exact dimensions.

When the excavation is completed, the walls are installed on earth shelves cut around the edge of the hole and joined with angle irons or some other means of fastening. To give them rigidity, A-frame braces are installed behind them.

When walls are secure, various cuts are made in them to accommodate the filter and coping.

After the walls are checked for squareness, sand (or peat moss) is dumped into the excavation, distributed evenly over the bottom with a rake, then tamped solidly in place after being sprayed lightly with a hose to give it body. The hopper—or deep part—of the pool is finished with a trowel.

Next, it's simply a matter of unrolling the vinyl liner into the excavation. The liner may be smoothed by hand, or a vacuum is used to suck out the air under it and pull it taut and smooth against the base.

After the coping is installed, the ladders and any other accessories go in. Final step is to install the filter. No. The final step is to fill the pool with water and jump in!

One note of caution when buying any pool. The industry is not devoid of sharp operators. It's best to deal with ones that are members of the National Swimming Pool Institute. Also, carefully check the guarantee you get with your pool. On more than one occasion, above-ground pools—wood or metal walls—have been known to buckle. If there isn't any guarantee, avoid it like the plague. And, do maintain your pool. If you see any rotting on wood or rusting-out on metal, check the pool inside and out—and do something about it immediately. Rot and rust are usually the causes of pool failure.

While pools are inviting in daytime (below) don't forget you can do nocturnal bathing also.

A PLACE FOR YOUR CAR

A carport provides full shelter for a car, and it's easy to build.

If you don't have a sheltered spot for your car, a carport may be just what you need. It provides adequate shelter for the automobile and, if you wish, you can build one with storage units. And the cost will be lots less than you'd pay for a garage.

THREE CARPORTS

Following are American Plywood Association designs for building three different carports. Number 1 is a simple one that has one main goal: To provide shelter for your car. Number 2 has two purposes: shelter for the car, and storage. The latter is large enough to house bulky items such as screens, bicycles and refuse cans. Smaller cabinets are for tools and cleaning equipment. The garden-side closet is big enough to hold wheelbarrow and fertilizer. You can build it attached to the house or free-standing.

Number 3 can have three purposes: car shelter, storage and the overhanging roof can serve as a sun cover for an adjacent patio.

While it protects your family car, a carport can also free garage space for many other uses.

CARPORT #1

Before you begin construction, it is recommended that you level the area over which the carport will be built. Then set eight foundation blocks in place to support the 4x4 inch posts, and level the blocks. Order Bowman (or equal) post brackets cast in concrete blocks from your dealer, or cast Bowman (or equal) post brackets in pre-mixed concrete yourself.

FRAMING MEMBERS

On a flat surface, build the four "H" frames by bolting a 4x4-inch post to each end of two 2x12-inch roof framing support members. (For maximum rigidity, drill all bolt holes in 4x4's the exact size as bolt diameter.) On one "H" frame "end section," bolt two 2x8-inch cabinet supports. (See drawing for details.)

When "H" frames are completed, tip the "H" frame "end section" into place and bolt to post brackets in foundation blocks. (For temporary bracing, support this and succeeding "H" frames to the ground with diagonal bracing.) Raise the three remaining "H" frames and secure in place. Then bolt the two 2x12-inch longitudinal roof framing supports to the 4x4-inch posts as shown in the drawing.

Cut the 2x6-inch roof joists to length, place them on top of the longitudinal stiffeners 16-inches on center, and toenail in place. Apply roof perimeter blocking and nail securely.

COVERING ROOF

Next, begin covering roof with plywood sheathing (plugged side up if Neoprene-Hypalon roof coating is used, otherwise C-C grade plywood may be used). Place plywood over joists so plywood's face grain runs perpendicular to joists, space panel edges 1/8-inch apart and ends 1/16-inch apart, and stagger panel end joints across the roof. Space nails 12-inches apart on interior of panel, and 6-inches apart at panel perimeter.

Apply cant-strip to roof, and plywood fascia to perimeter of carport roof deck. Be certain to nail plywood fascia to cant-strip on roof, and to 2x6-inch joists and blocking, and to 2x12-inch longitudinal roof framing for strength.

Carport Number 1 has one main goal: to shelter car. It's easiest of carports to make.

DRAINAGE

Install facilities for drainage. (See your dealer for scuppers, down-spouts and related materials.) Then apply Neoprene-Hypalon roof coating, or use built-up roofing materials and apply metal roof trim.

Finish the carport with paint or stain, as desired.

Finally, install the three storage cabinets to face inside or outside the carport, or alternate them. (See storage cabinet construction details.)

CARPORT #1

Foundation Layout

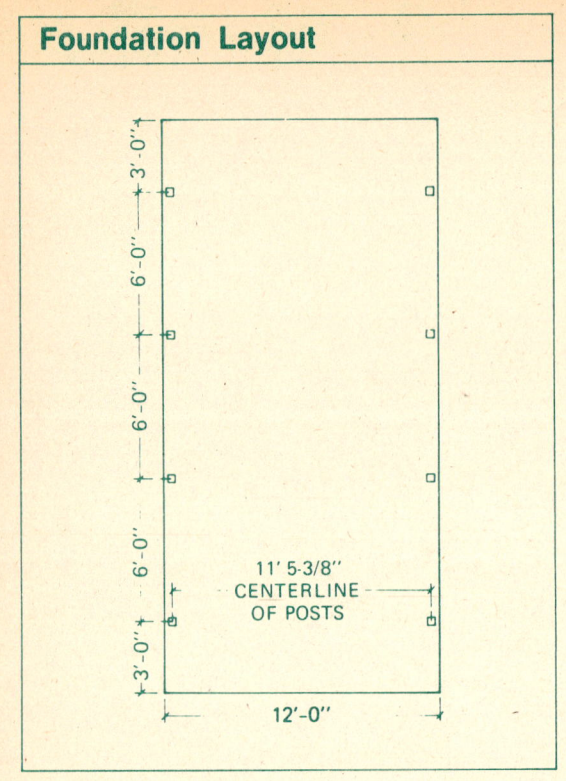

3'-0"
6'-0"
6'-0"
6'-0"
3'-0"

11' 5-3/8" CENTERLINE OF POSTS

12'-0"

Section A

3/8" EXT DFPA TEXTURED PLYWOOD
METAL FLASHING
2 x 4 BEVELED AS SHOWN
3/8" C-C (PLUGGED) EXT DFPA PLYWOOD
2 x 6 BLOCKING
2 x 6 JOIST
1/2" DIA. BOLTS W/ WASHERS
2 x 12
2 x 12 LATERAL BRACES
1/2" DIA. BOLTS W/ WASHERS
4 x 4 POST
7'-0"
1/2" DIA. BOLTS W/ WASHERS
1"
BOWMAN FASTENER PRE CAST IN CONCRETE BLOCKS

Front Elevation

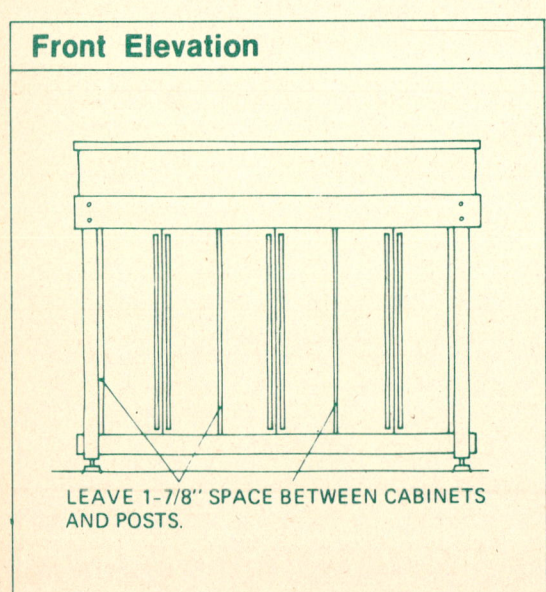

LEAVE 1-7/8" SPACE BETWEEN CABINETS AND POSTS.

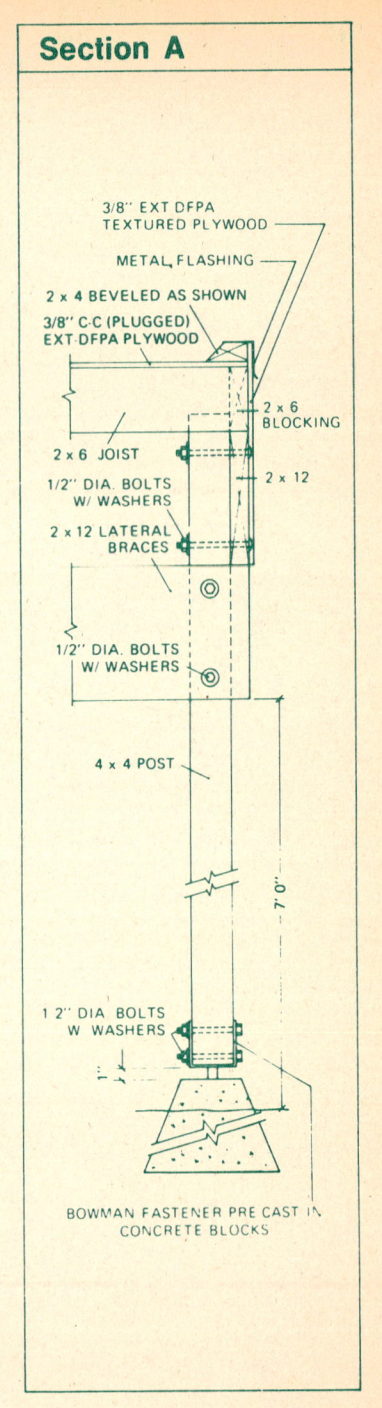

CARPORT #2

Excavate trenches for footings and walls to required depth below frost line. Construct formwork to dimensions shown and pour concrete. Note that front and end walls on both left and right, and the wing wall are 1⅝-inches lower for plates to form a base. Drill holes for anchor bolts and set these lower plates as shown.

Cut wall framing, including wing wall, to length and assemble in sections on a flat surface and then raise into place, one at a time. The rear plates are fastened with anchor bolts. The front plates are nailed to lower plates already in position with a ¾-inch off-set to provide doorsteps at the bottom. Plumb framing with carpenter's level and nail sections into place as shown. Now install shelf supports in left cabinet.

Cut plywood walls and doors to fit. Install shelf and inside plywood partitions and then nail plywood panels into place with 8d box or casing nails spaced 6-inches at panel edges. Note that upper panel at right end must be notched for rafters.

RAFTERS

Cut rafters to length and install over cabinets with rafters nailed to house studs as shown in detail; then apply 1x6-inch fascia board. Install ½-inch exterior plywood roof sheathing over, using 6d common nails spaced 6-inches at panel edges and 12-inches along intermediate rafters. Lay roll roofing over plywood using metal flashing at the house wall and carport roof to prevent leakage.

Next, fit and hang ¾-inch plywood doors using 6-inch galvanized T-hinges. Provide a 2x2-inch stop along meeting edge of one of each pair of doors. Install safety hasps as shown in detail. When pouring the carport floor, set bolts for fastening 2x4-inch wheel stop, if desired.

FINISH

Stain or paint may be used for protection against weather. Two coats of an exterior quality opaque oil stain or shingle paint are preferred for lasting beauty and minimum maintenance. If a paint finish is desired, for the first coat, apply a high grade exterior primer with a heavy application to plywood edges. Follow with two coats of a good quality house paint, being certain to apply equal coats to fronts and backs of doors.

CARPORT #3

If you have no patio, and no carport, this combination carport/patio shelter

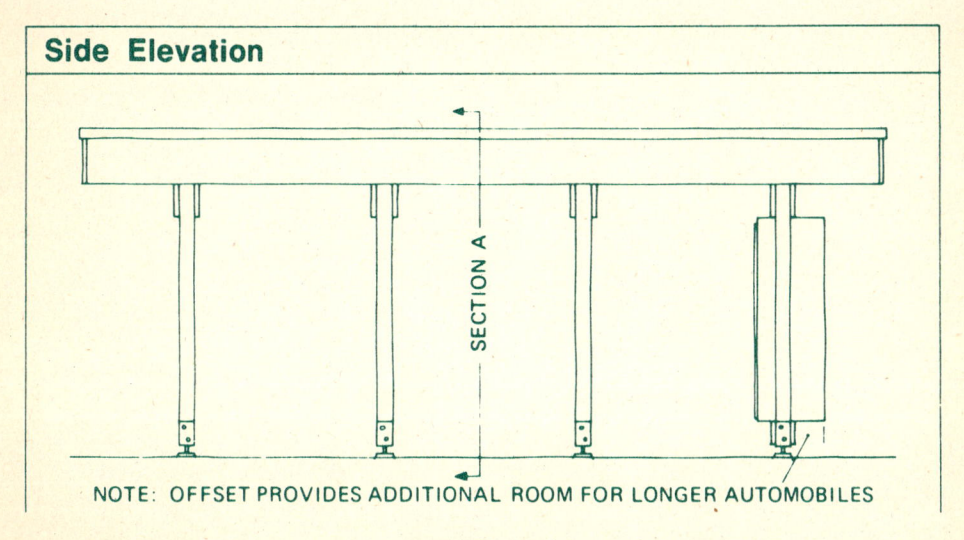

Side Elevation

SECTION A

NOTE: OFFSET PROVIDES ADDITIONAL ROOM FOR LONGER AUTOMOBILES

CARPORT #1

Fabrication Sequence

CABINET SUPPORT RAILS
H FRAME

CARPORT #1

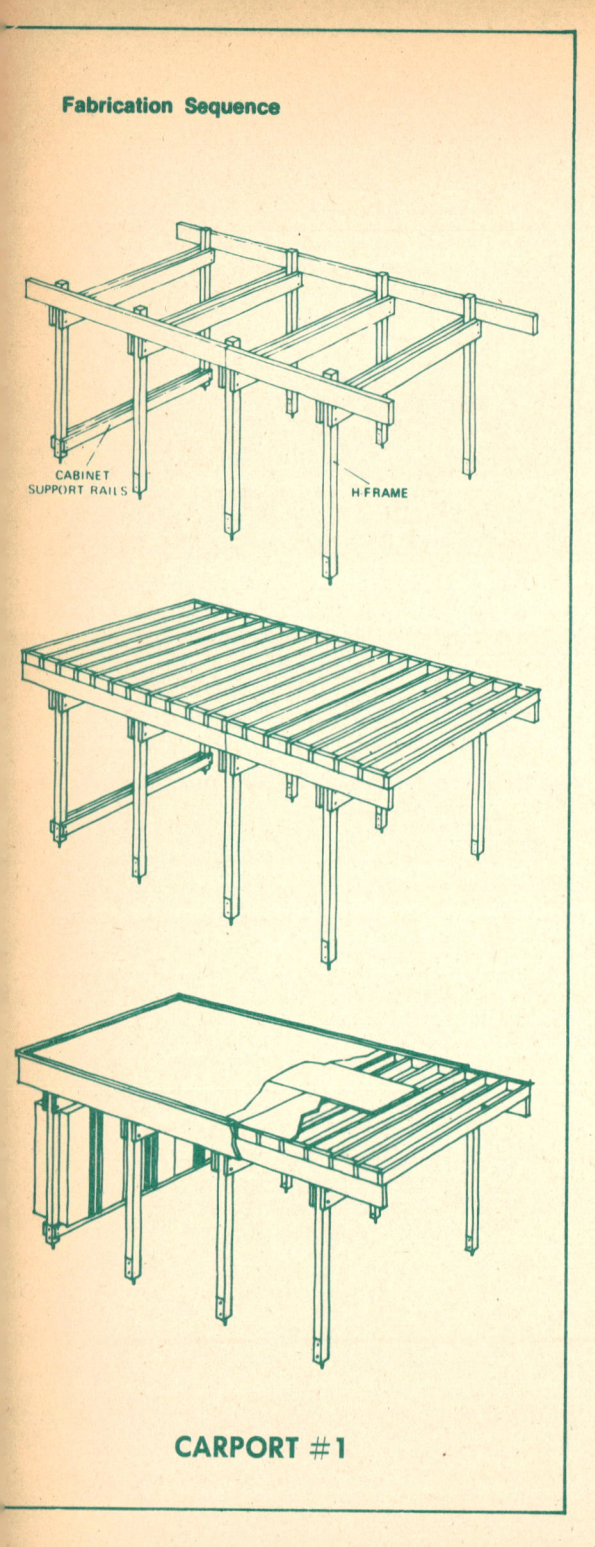

could be just what you need. But the design is adaptable. If you do have a patio and its location is practical, you can build the carport and the shelter roof to extend over the existing patio. On the other hand, you may just choose to build the carport, forgetting the extension. Here, we show how to build the complete structure—carport and shelter roof.

The carport and patio are built on a concrete slab, with the patio portion segmented into 4-foot squares with cedar strips, or screeds.

FOUNDATION

Begin by laying out the location of post and wall footings. Stake out the corners and intersections of post footings with rear wall and edge of slab in front. Check for square by measuring diagonally from corner to corner. When dimensions are the same on each diagonal, the building is in square. Now dig a 2-foot wide trench to a depth below local frost line for the foundation wall that runs along the rear and right side. Dig 2-foot square holes at each post footing location.

Next, set batter boards approximately 2-feet out from corners and the intersection of the post line with rear wall and front edge of slab. Stretch strings to locate outside face of foundation wall and post line. Check for square again.

SETTING FORMS

Stake 2x6's on edge for footings along the rear and right side. Build wall forms for foundation to the required height with 2x4's and plywood or shiplap. Set outside form panels on top edge of 2x6 footing forms and nail into position with inside face lined up with batter board strings. Set inside form panels so that forms are 6-inches apart. Install one row of form ties about halfway up from top of footing and nail wood bracing on 2x4's across the top where required. Install wood spreaders between forms as needed. Build bottomless boxes for post footings from 2x6 scrap lumber. Assemble 6-inch x 6-inch plinth forms from scrap shiplap and nail to 2x4's fastened across post footing forms. Pour concrete into forms, then insert shop-

CARPORT #2

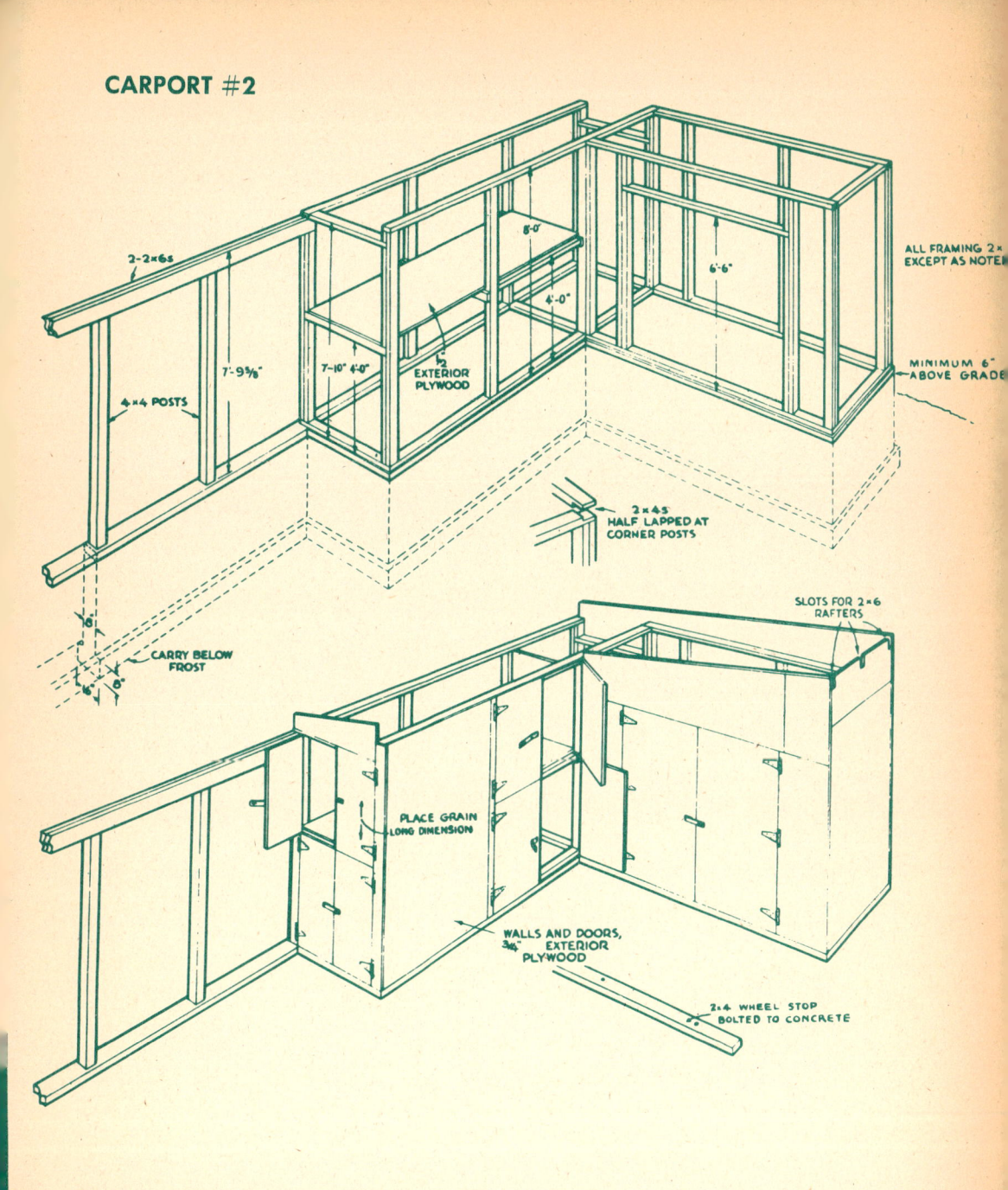

CARPORT #2

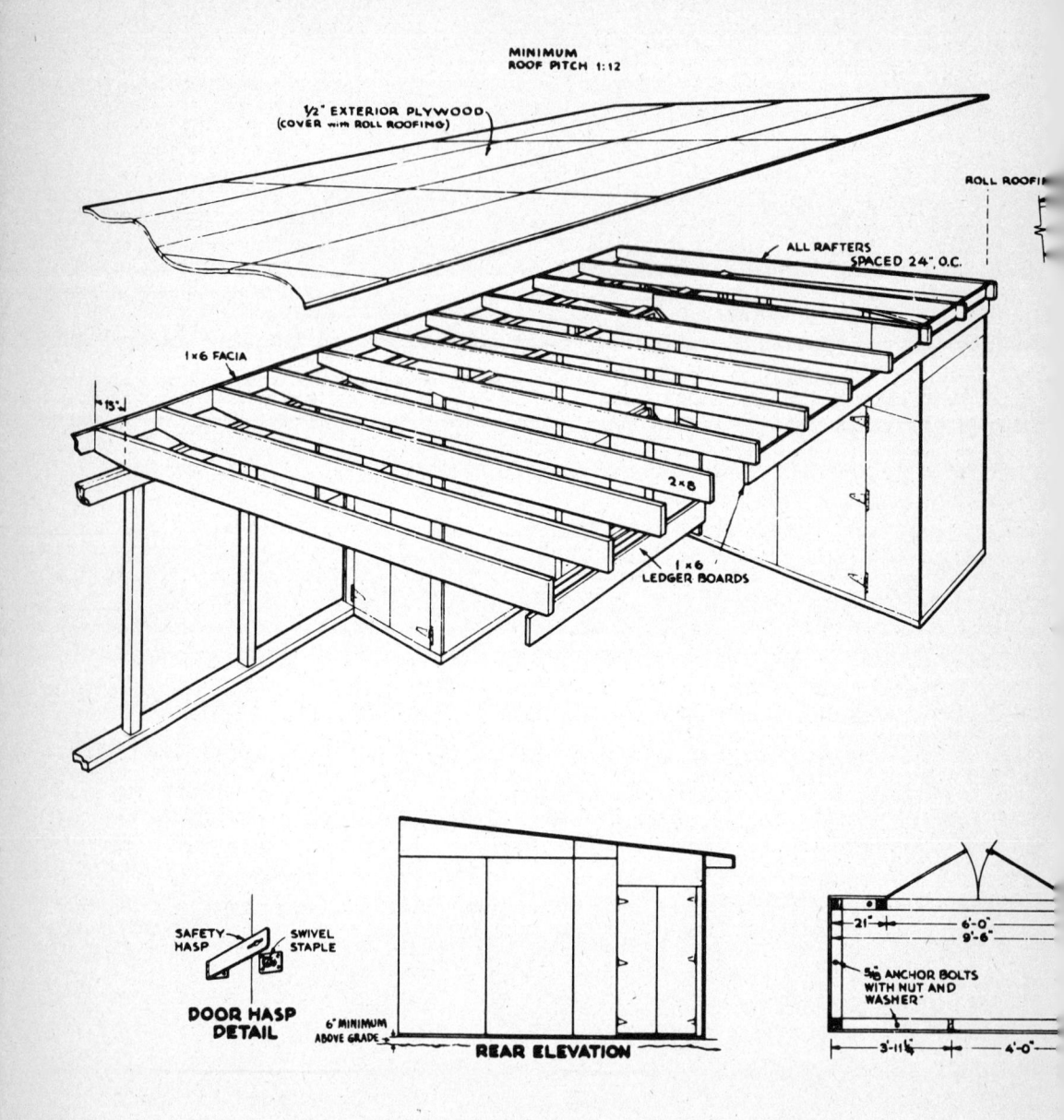

PLAN

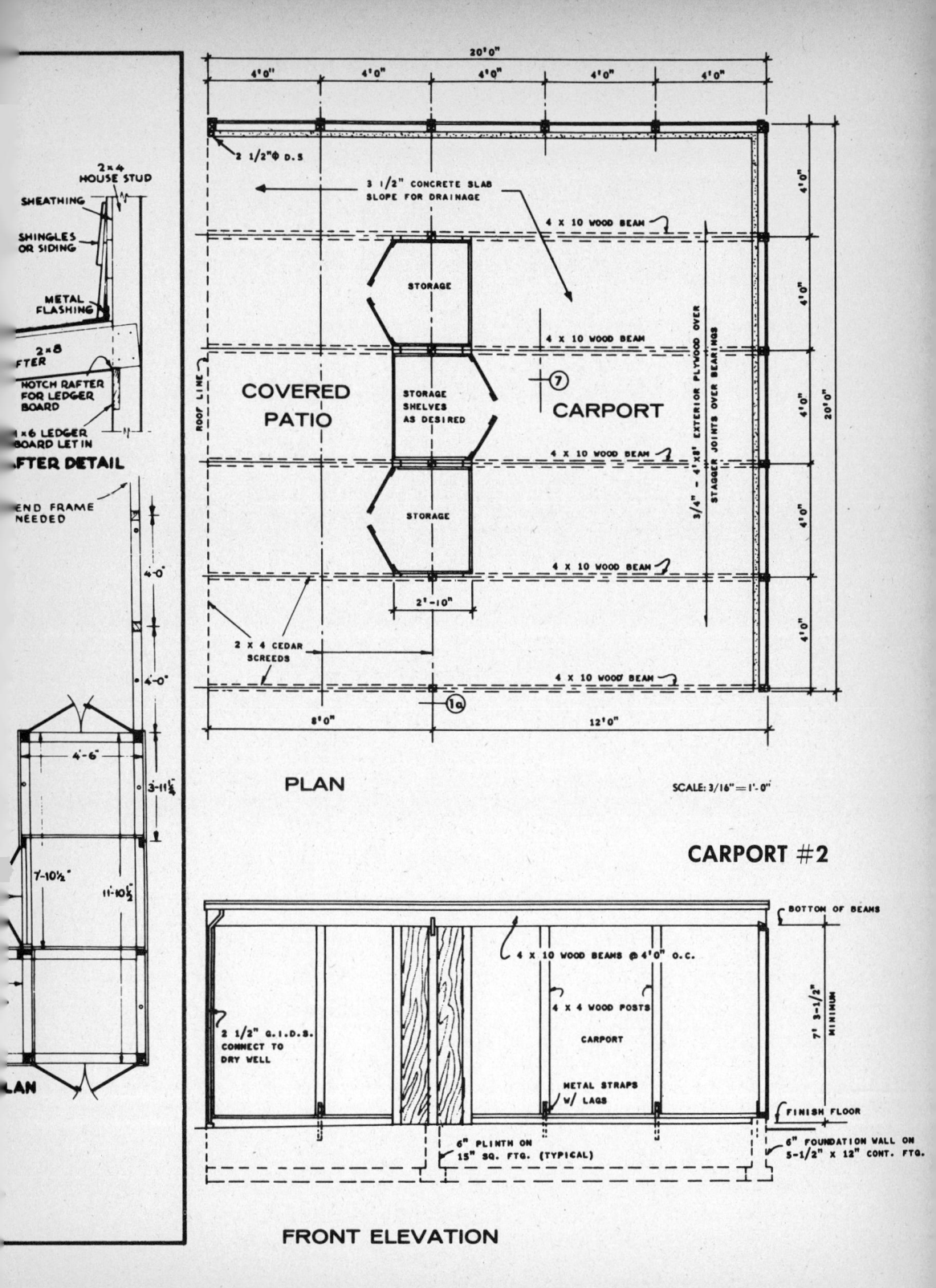

SCALE: 3/16" = 1'-0"

CARPORT #2

FRONT ELEVATION

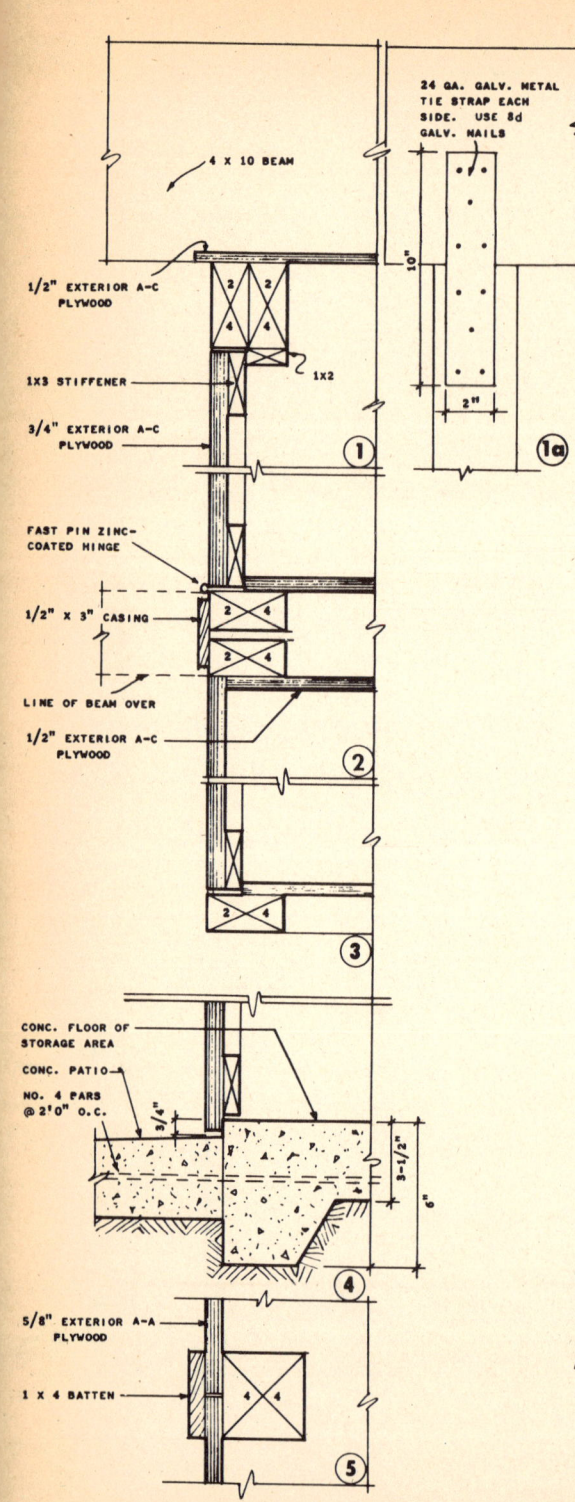

primed 1/8 x 2 x 16-inch metal scraps into the concrete foundation at each post location. Insert double straps into plinths at each post footing. Treat 2x4 plates with toxic water repellent. Using a carpenter's level, set plates on top of freshly poured wall with 20d nails driven into bottom side to act as plate anchors.

INSTALLING POSTS

Remove formwork after concrete has sufficiently hardened. Cut 4-inch x 4-inch posts to length, fasten with ½-inch lags to metal strips holding them upright with temporary diagonal braces to the 2x4 plate on foundation walls. Also, position and fasten posts to straps from footing plinths. Now nail a 2x4 continuous plate across the posts on the right carport wall. Cut 4x10-inch beams to length and fasten to top plate with metal joist anchors on both sides of each beam. Use galvanized metal tie straps and nails in other locations where beams are connected directly to posts. Keep beams aligned with temporary bracing across the tops. It would be well at this stage of construction to apply two coats of stain to all the beams, posts and plates.

Prime both sides and edges of the exterior plywood wall panels before installation. When primer is dry, fasten to posts, plates and beams with 8d non-rusting box or casing nails, 6-inches on center along all edges. Use ¾-inch exterior plywood for roof.

CARPORT #3

WALTER D. WIDMEYER ARCHITECT

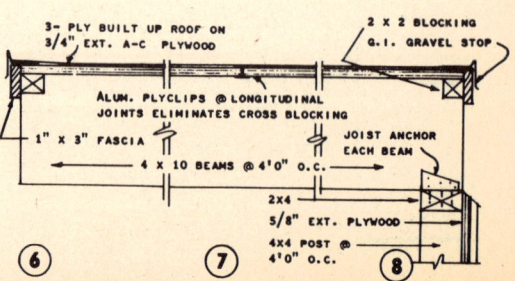

DOOR & SCREEN DETAILS SCALE: 1-1/2" = 1'-0"

ROOF DETAILS SCALE: 3/4" = 1'-0"

CARPORT #3

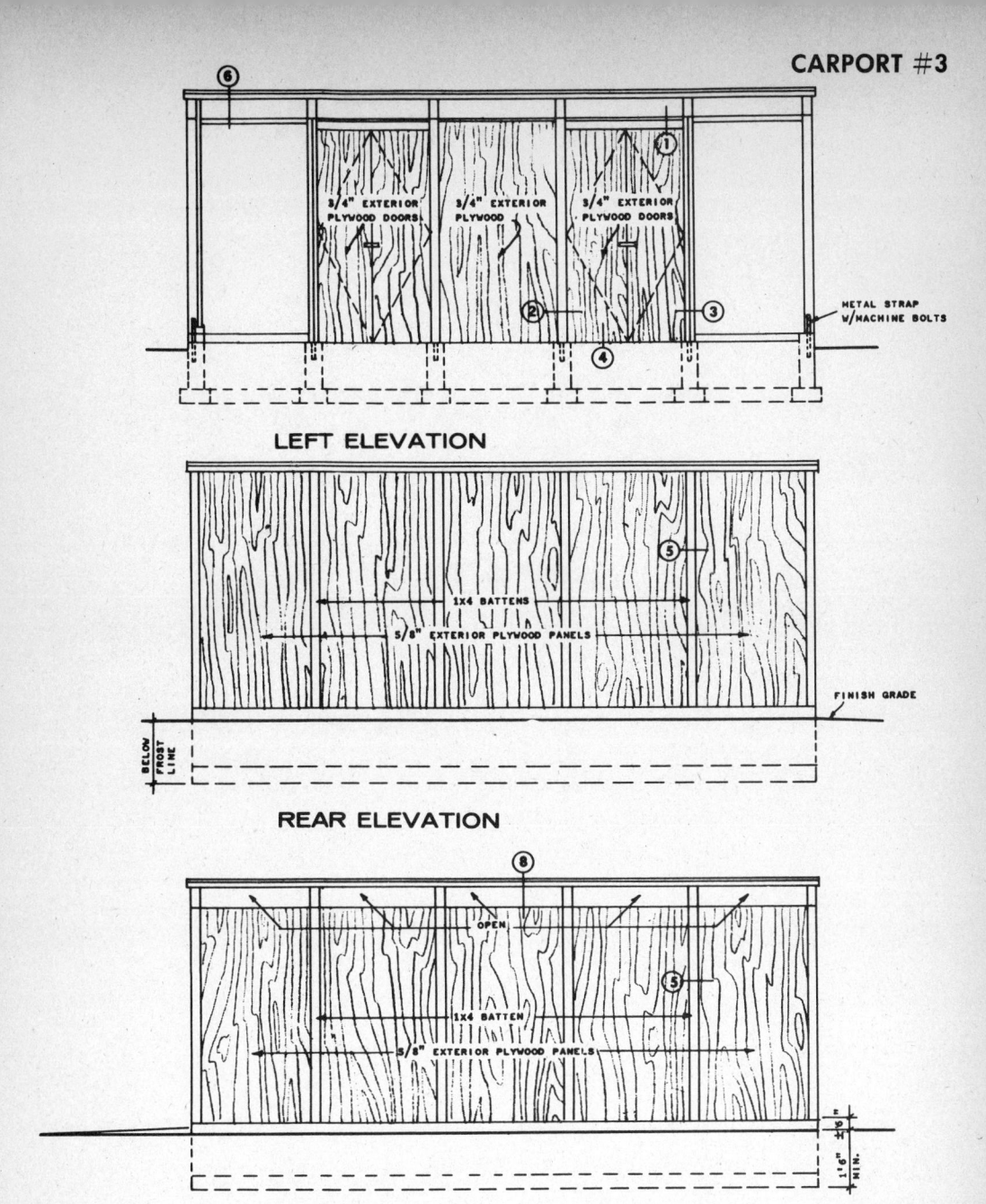

LEFT ELEVATION

REAR ELEVATION

RIGHT ELEVATION

After applying a coat of primer to the "A" face and edges of the panels, fasten them to the tops of the beams with end edges staggered. Use aluminum ply-clips (available at lumberyards) on 16-inch centers and fasten panels with 8d common nails 6-inches on center along edges at bearings. Install 2x2 blocking between beams at outside edges to provide nailing for the 1x3-inch V.G. Fir fascia which should be back primed before installation. Set galvanized shop-primed nipple and base plate for 2½-inch diameter downspout.

Portland Cement Assn.

Steps needn't be conventional. Concrete rounds provide beautiful accent to sloping terrain.

ABC'S OF BUILDING STEPS

Whether you build one step or a few, it's easy if you're careful.

Outdoor projects sometimes involve building steps. Steps that lead from the back of the house to the patio, deck steps, entrance steps. Or perhaps, you may just want to install new steps to replace ones you have now.

There are two kinds you can make: wood and concrete. Of the two, wood are easiest to make. Before beginning, you should consider what size the steps should be.

STEP DIMENSIONS

In the first place, they must conform to local building code requirements. Steps for private homes are usually 48-inches wide, though some codes allow 30 and 36-inch widths. Steps should be at least as wide as the door and walk they serve.

A landing is desirable to divide flights of more than 5-feet and it should be no shorter than 3-feet. The top landing should

BUILDING A SINGLE STEP

SIMPLE WOOD STEPS

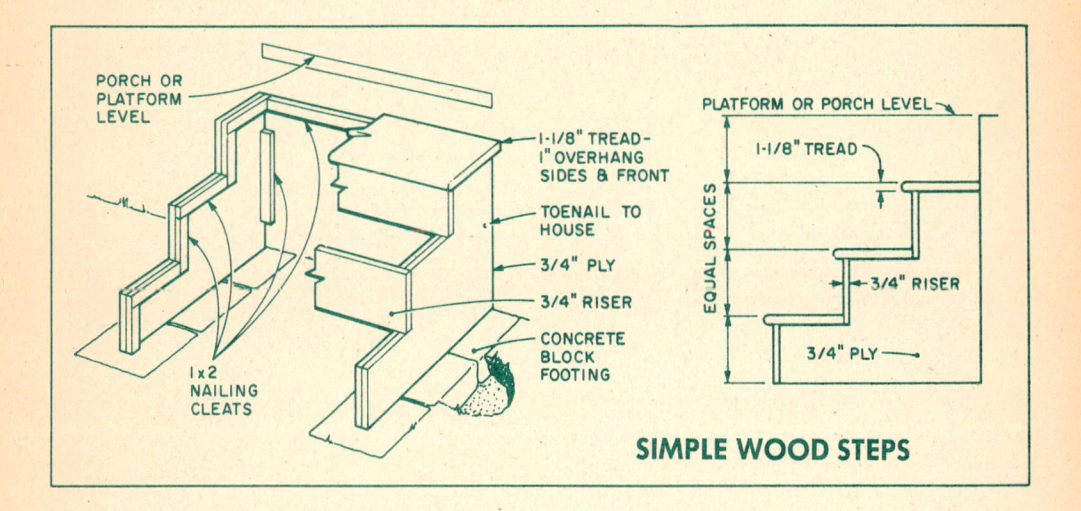

be no more than 7½-inches below the door threshold.

For flights less than 30-inches high, maximum step rise is usually 7½-inches, and minimum tread width, 11-inches. For higher flights, step rise may be limited to 6-inches, with a minimum tread width of 12-inches. Choice of riser and tread size should depend on how steps are to be used. For esthetic reasons, steps with risers as low as 4-inches and treads as wide as 19-inches are often built. On long, sloping approaches, a stepped ramp can be used.

Many studies have been made to find the best size combination of riser and tread for comfort and safety. One study concludes that the sum of riser and tread should equal 17½-inches. This is a good combination for most steps. However, around the garden-patio area more generous steps, usually for good looks, can be used. Here, the following combinations of riser to tread dimensions can be used: 4 to 19, 4½ to 18, 5 to 17, 5½ to 16, or 6 to 15-inches.

As a general rule, the closer the steps come to normal walking stride, the safer and easier it is for all ages. For safety you shouldn't vary the height of risers and the width of treads in any one flight.

BUILDING A SINGLE STEP

The patio is often not level with the house floor level, and one or more steps can make life easier for everyone. Putting in a concrete one is good here. You can use a pre-mixed concrete, such as Sakrete —all you do is add water as if baking a cake—in specified proportions.

You can pour the concrete step directly on firm earth. Use smooth 2x6 or 2x8 forms, depending on height of step wanted. Form as shown and brace well, using carpenter's level for accuracy. Slope away from house at the rate of ⅛-inch per foot.

CONCRETE STEPS

ISOLATION JOINT

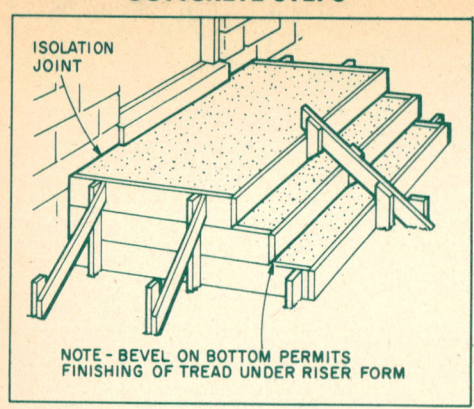

NOTE - BEVEL ON BOTTOM PERMITS FINISHING OF TREAD UNDER RISER FORM

After pouring the concrete mix, tamp into place, then rough-level with a straight board or screed. Rest screed on form and move forward in a sawing motion. Round edges of step with edging tool.

A half-hour or more after screeding, as cement begins to set, finish surface with wood float for a non-skid texture; use steel trowel for smooth finish. Use a half-arc motion under light pressure. Re-edge with edging tool. Cure concrete by covering it with wet paper, burlap or cloth the second day after pouring. Keep concrete damp for one week.

If you have a need for a short flight of steps—say two or three—wood ones can serve you well.

SIMPLE WOOD STEPS

First step here, as it were, is to decide how many steps you need. While we mentioned before that 7½-inches is a good height for a riser, it could really range from between 6½ to 8½-inches, with the treads each an inch or two longer than each riser.

To find this out, measure from floor level to ground level. Let's say that the result is 24-inches. If you divide that by 8, which would be an 8-inch riser height falling between the acceptable 6½ to 8½-inch riser height—that means that you'll need three risers and two steps.

Once you have these dimensions, allow 1¼-inch thickness for tread, and cut the end support walls to size from ¾-inch exterior fir plywood. Fasten 1x2 blocks to near top edge of end supports to fasten treads and risers to.

Now, cut treads long enough so they are 2-inches longer than length across stairs and overlap an inch on each side. Use 1¼-inch yellow pine stair tread (stock item at lumberyards) and ¾-inch exterior plywood for risers.

With the steps made, excavate the area they'll occupy to the width and depth of a cement block (4-inchesx8-inches), then set the blocks (each 16-inches long) end-to-end in this mini-trench to serve as your footings. Paint the steps the color of the house trim (or whatever you wish), set them in place and toenail them to the house—one nail on each side.

CONCRETE STEPS

The most challenging steps for the handyman to build are concrete ones of any appreciable rise. It takes muscle and great care.

FOOTINGS

Concrete steps require footings. The following economical trick will prevent their sinking. Two or more 6 to 8-inch diameter postholes should be dug beneath the bottom tread and filled with concrete, with holes extending at least 6-inches below frost line. Also, tie the top step or landing to the foundation wall with two or more metal anchors.

FORMS

When building forms, brace them rigidly to prevent bulging and leaking. The boards should be straight, and free from imperfections that would be visible in the hardened concrete.

Start installation of riser forms at the top. Check with a hand level to allow ¼-inch slope on each tread for drainage. A bevel on the lower edge of the form will permit finishing the full tread width. As mentioned, brace the forms well. Wood cleats are the best way to attach riser forms to plywood sidewall forms (see illustration). Use wood wedges to hold risers between solid concrete or masonry walls. Braces are usually centered on the risers and staked and nailed outside the formwork.

During forming, allow for any recesses needed for attachment of ironwork or railings. Also, an "isolation" joint is required where the top tread or landing meets the building. A thin layer of building paper will do the job. If this is not done, the concrete may bond to the wall and some day cause a crack.

FILL MATERIALS

Brick, stone, or broken concrete can be used inside the formwork as fill to reduce the amount of concrete needed. Don't have any fill material any closer than 4-inches from the face of any form.

CONCRETE

You can use the same concrete mix for steps as for driveways, sidewalks, and patios, except that the maximum size of coarse aggregate should not exceed 1-inch.

Before pouring the concrete, wet forms with water or oil. Forms to be removed the same day can be wetted with water; those to stay in place several days should be oiled.

After concrete has set up, carefully remove forms. See text on how to finish them well.

Start pouring with the bottom step and work upward filling against sidewall forms as work progresses. Spade or vibrate the concrete, especially next to form faces. Float off each step as it is filled. Finally, tap forms lightly to release air bubbles.

FINISHING STEPS

There are a few ways to do this. One good way is as follows. Strike off, darby and edge the landing and the top step. Then hand-float it and give it its first troweling. Next, do each step. Hand float tread and edge it along the riser form, allowing a ¼ to ½-inch radius. Wait until the steps are set sufficiently to hold their shape, then remove riser boards. Float the riser and use an inside step tool where the riser meets the tread below. The radius of this tool is usually the same as that used at the top of the riser.

If sufficient mortar cannot be worked out of the concrete for proper finishing, a little mortar consisting of one part cement to about 1½ parts fine sand should be applied. After troweling, draw a damp brush across the riser and get a fine-textured, nonslip surface. Repeat for each riser. Fast and careful work is essential since too much time on any one step may cause the others to set too firmly for proper finishing.

Remove side forms the same day, float them, then plaster with ⅛ to ¼-inch layer of mortar. Spread the mortar with a trowel, then float it with a cork or sponge rubber float. This finish is suitable for most step sidewalls. If a smooth finish is desired, troweling should follow. A brushed or swirl finish may be used after floating or troweling.

Following this, let the concrete cure properly by keeping it wet for a week.

NON-SLIP FINISHES

Non-slip finishes for better safety on steps can be obtained in a number of ways. Brushing, swirl-floating, and swirl-troweling produce a rough texture, but these may wear smooth under heavy traffic. A more permanent non-slip tread can be gotten by using a dry-shake of abrasive grains such as silicon carbide or aluminum oxide. The most permanent non-slip steps are built with special abrasive strips and nosings that are embedded while the concrete treads are still wet.

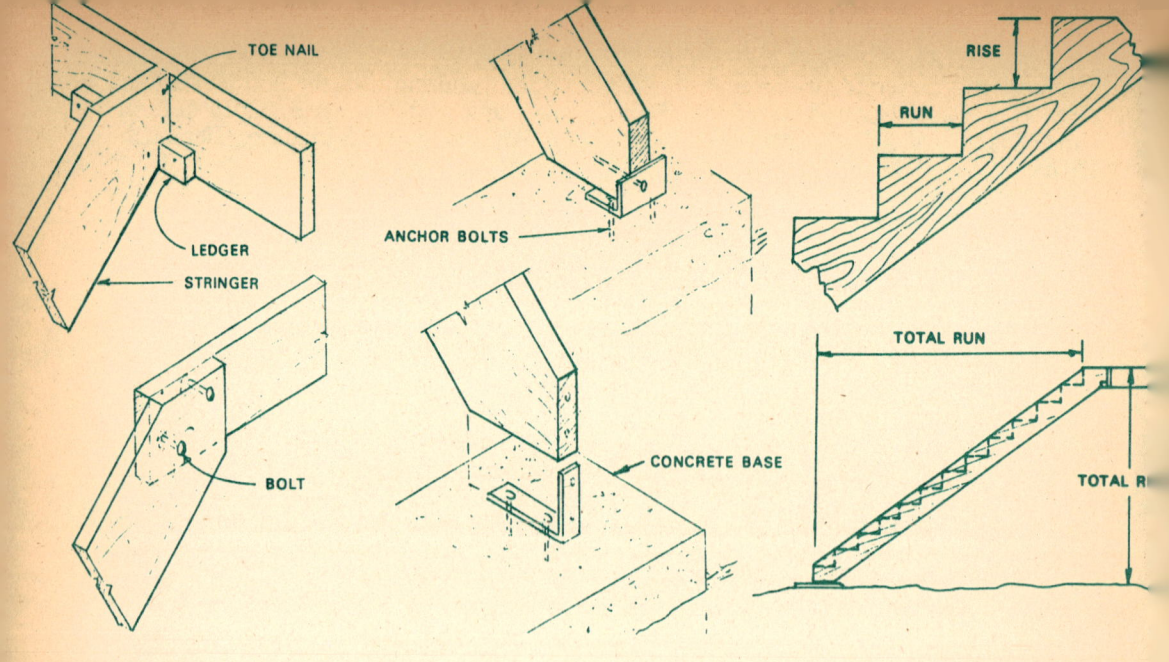

WOOD STAIRWAYS

It's almost always the case that decks require stairs. There's no great mystery in constructing them. They're much the same as inside stairs, except that construction details are used that are designed to avoid trapping moisture and using exposed end grain, which can also absorb moisture.

If you use wood that has low decay resistance for making stairs, a three-minute dip in a water repellent will triple their useful life.

STRINGERS

As with any steps, you have a variety of building options. The basic set of stairs consists of the stair stringer, or supporting side pieces, and the treads. Stringers should be used in pairs no more than 3-feet apart. They are usually made of 10-inch or 2x12-inch members. Stringers must be well secured to deck framing. They are normally supported by a ledger or by the extension of a joist or beam. The ledger can be a 2x3-inch or 2x4-inch piece secured to the framing bottom with 12d nails. The stringer is notched and rests on this.

Stair stringers can also be bolted to joist or beam ends when stringers are no more than 3-feet apart. Use at least two ½-inch galvanized bolts for fastening.

ANCHORING BOTTOM OF STRINGER

For maximum durability, the stringer ends should be anchored to a base set in the earth. Two methods for doing this are used. They can be secured to metal anchors set in a concrete base (angles should be thick enough to keep wood off concrete); concrete should be sloped for drainage. You can also fasten them to a treated wood member anchored in concrete or the ground.

TREADS AND RISERS

To determine riser and tread size, you can follow instructions previously given. Support for the treads can be accomplished in a variety of ways. You can cut dadoes into the sides of the stringers. Stringers can also be notched to form supports for treads and risers, if any. However both methods expose end grain and it's really best to avoid them.

A better method is to bolt 2x4 ledgers or supports to the stringers to support treads. Ledgers can be sloped back slightly so water will drain. They might also be beveled to minimize tread contact. Use 2x10 or 2x12 treads secured by three 12 d deformed shank nails at each stringer. You could also use 3-inch long rust-proof screws. Always place treads bark side up to prevent cupping and retention of water. If you wish, you can also make treads of 2x6, but the span must be limited to 42-inches for less dense woods.

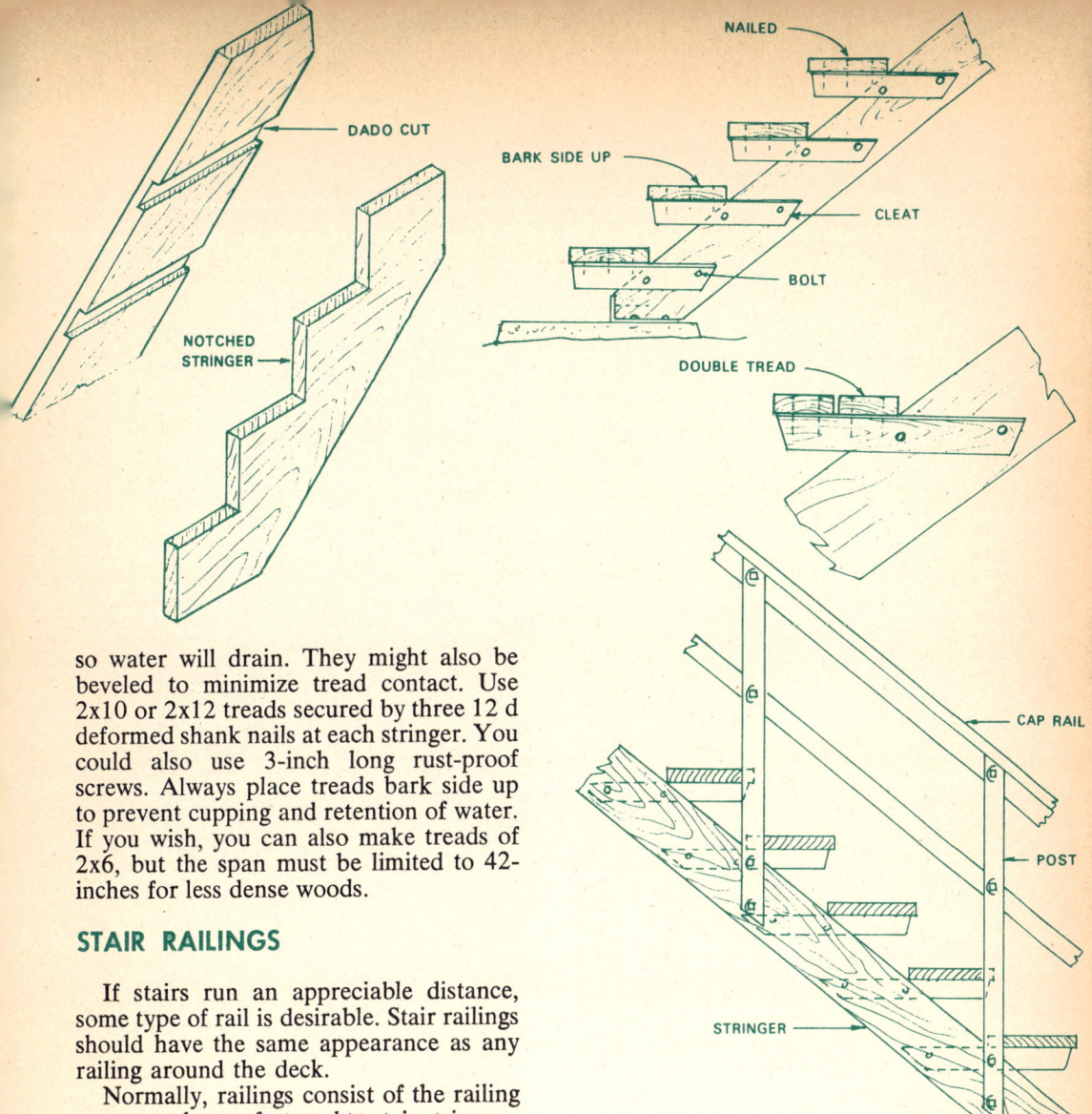

STAIR RAILINGS

If stairs run an appreciable distance, some type of rail is desirable. Stair railings should have the same appearance as any railing around the deck.

Normally, railings consist of the railing proper and posts fastened to stair stringers. There can be one railing on top of intermediate rails on the posts.

Size of members varies. When spacing is no more than 3-feet, posts can be 2x4's. When spacing is 3 to 6-feet, use 3x4 or 2x6 posts. Longitudinal cap, top and intermediate rails are usually 2x4's or wider. Nail the cap rail to the top rail with 12 d deformed shank nails spaced 12 to 16-inches.

Of course, many different rail designs are possible in addition to the two mentioned here. The main thing, other than harmony with the deck in terms of design, is that it be strong enough to do its job.

Finished concrete steps are as durable as they are good looking. Good finishing is key.

A NEW DRIVEWAY

If your driveway is cracked, here's how to solve the problem for good.

If your driveway has so many cracks that it looks like a jigsaw puzzle, a new driveway is called for. Two kinds are common: asphalt and concrete, with concrete the way to go for the do-it-yourselfer. To do a proper job with asphalt you need a steamroller, which is simply impractical.

REMOVE OLD CONCRETE

First step in installing a new driveway is to break up and remove all the old concrete down to bare earth. There is no easy way to do this: it's hard work. But there are a couple of tricks to minimize the muscle output.

The job is done with a sledgehammer. Pick one that's not too heavy for you. They come in various sizes, starting at around 6 pounds and going up in two-pound increments.

To use the hammer, raise it and let it fall of its own weight on the concrete; don't drive it. Aim for the edges of the pieces, rather than the middle, breaking off small, manageable chunks.

If while chopping you come across tree roots, cut *completely* through them with a saw and discard. Roots are common culprits in making a concrete driveway crack.

Before you start breaking up the concrete, you should arrange for getting rid of the broken pieces. If you have an old cesspool, fine. You can just haul the pieces to it (by wheelbarrow, to minimize the work) and fill it up. If you are going to haul it away yourself, it's a good idea to pull the truck (don't use a car; it won't bear the weight) up as close to the driveway as possible. If you have no way of removing the material yourself you can hire someone to carry it away.

FORMS

After the concrete is hauled away, it's time to build forms for the new driveway. These are simply 2x4's, set on both sides of the driveway. They do three things: retain the concrete, and establish its outer edge and top.

Use straight 2x4's for the job; warped ones will cause problems.

First, assuming you want the same size driveway as before, use a spade to cut away the sod on both sides of the driveway—from street (or sidewalk) to garage floor—to the thickness of a 2x4. Following Figure, set mason's guidelines with string, then stake the forms in place. The forms should be placed so that their top edges run about ½-inch below ground level, except at the street end, where they should be flush and the garage end, where they should be 1-inch or so lower than the floor. This extra drop will keep water out of the garage.

A new driveway can add immeasurably to the good looks of your house. But build it strong.

To set the boards properly, you'll have to remove or pack dirt under the boards. Also, as you go, remember that the 2x4's must pitch downward (for drainage). If necessary you can bend them as needed just before you stake them in place.

If your driveway is curved, it's better to pour it in two or three sections, using straight forms, rather than try to bend or cut the forms to achieve a perfectly curved shape. Of course, if you are experienced at this type of thing, then by all means do it.

MAKING THE DRIVEWAY

Now, you're ready to get into the heart of making the driveway. The one described here is designed to eliminate the possibility of cracking, so you don't have to go through the procedure again in four or five years.

First, dig out the ground to a depth of 6-inches—i.e., from the top of the form boards. After digging carefully, smooth out the dirt with a large rake.

Have your mason supply dealer deliver enough bankrun (sand) to cover the driveway to a depth of 2-inches. Spread it all over, then use a screed (see sketch for how to build one) to level it out to the required 2-inches. Best way to use the screed is to grip it in the middle and push it back and forth as if removing excess frosting from a cake.

Next, purchase enough wire mesh reinforcing (this is wire about $1/8$-inch thick in 6-inch squares). Using tinsnips, cut it into various size pieces to fit the driveway, then lay it aside in the positions it will go in.

1. First step in creating driveway: excavate to proper depth. Get all green matter out.

2. Set form boards, aligning the tops with a mason's string. Stake boards in place.

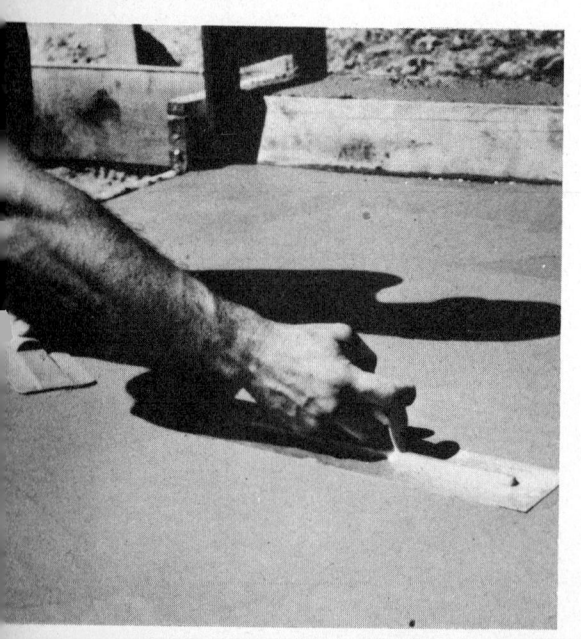

5. If you're handy, you can get a nice finish job with steel trowel, but it takes practice.

6. Initial smoothing of concrete can be done with bull nose float. Wield it carefully.

3. Use sharpened stakes to lock form boards in place. Concrete exerts considerable force.

4. Pour concrete, in two stages, after first laying sand base. Level concrete with forms.

POURING THE CONCRETE

Next step is to pour the concrete. You can mix your own, but it is much easier, even cheaper, to have it delivered by a mixed-in-transit truck.

The concrete is poured in two stages, each time to a 2-inch depth, forming a 4-inch slab. After the first batch is poured, screed it off to the 2-inch depth (wear rubber boots so you can walk right in the concrete). After the 2-inches are in, place the pieces of wire mesh on top. For every 30-feet of driveway—and this includes the garage floor which becomes part of the total slab—you should have an expansion joint. This is simply a piece of asphalt impregnated material that is cut to extend across the driveway from form to form and 4-inches high. If it happens that the joint falls somewhere in the middle of the driveway, back it up with a 2x4 before you make the final 2-inch pour. Otherwise the cement can knock it over. Expansion joints, by the way, let the concrete expand and contract without cracking and are very necessary.

Make your final 2-inch pour, screeding it level with the tops of the forms.

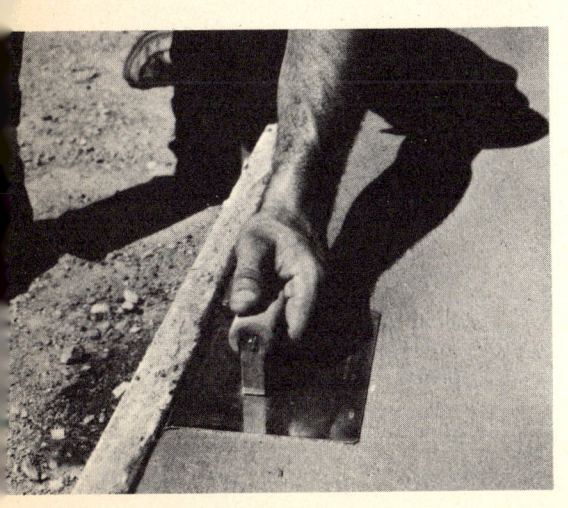

Special edging tool can be bought. It does neat job where concrete marries with forms.

MAKING THE DRIVEWAY

Diagram labels:
- 2" CONCRETE - FIRST POUR
- 2" CONCRETE - FINAL POUR
- 6" WIRE MESH
- USE STAKES & MASON STRING TO GET PITCH OF 1/8" IN 10'
- MASON STRING
- STAKE
- 2" SAND
- 6"
- 2x4 FORM
- SMOOTH EARTH
- SCREED - USE TO LEVEL VARIOUS LAYERS
- TEMPORARY 2x4 & STAKES
- EXPANSION JOINT
- PREVIOUSLY POURED CONCRETE

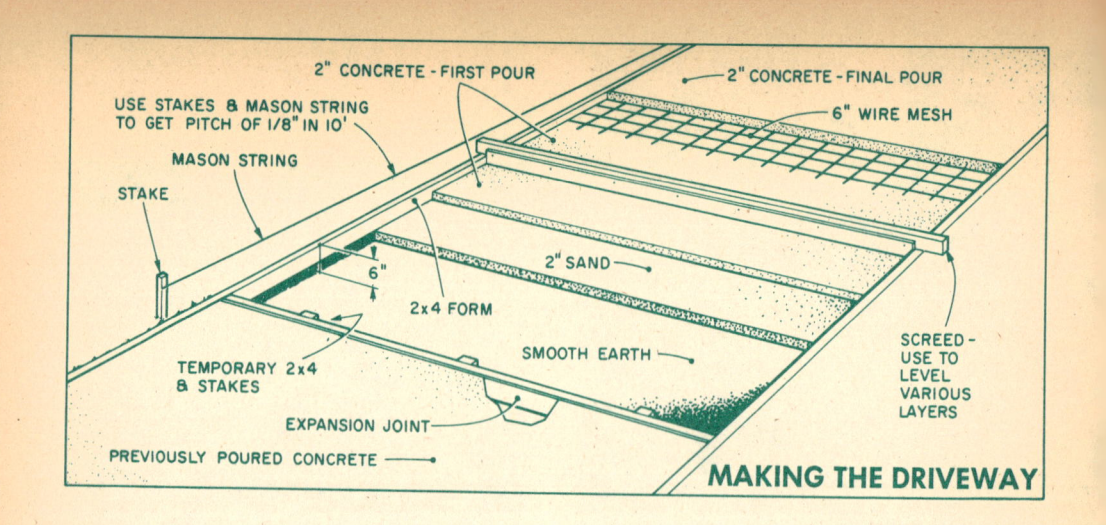

FINISHING OFF THE CONCRETE

Finishing off the concrete is the point where some skill is needed. If you have never done any finishing, you might practice a bit on a small job before launching into installing the driveway. If you don't feel that you'll be able to do it, it is a simple matter to hire a mason for just the finishing. It will only take him a short amount of time and will insure a good job.

At any rate, there are two ways to finish the concrete: with a steel trowel or a float. The former will produce a smooth surface, the latter a rough.

To use either, you have to do the job—catch the concrete—at the right moment. That is, when it's neither too wet or too dry. If it's too wet the float or trowel will "dig" holes too easily, too hard and you'll have to press too hard.

Try to catch the concrete after all the water has disappeared from the surface. If using a steel trowel, make sweeping, semicircular passes with the front or leading edge of the trowel raised. You needn't raise the float edge, but do also make semicircular passes. When the main sections are done, run over the edges with an edging tool to round them off.

Pretty driveway is made by pouring concrete with colorful aggregate, then exposing.

Screed is used to level sand, then concrete when making driveway. Use straight boards.

If you want to make a curved driveway, bend boards as shown. Use green lumber for job.

When finishing is complete, wait until the concrete is hard (the next day), then wet it down with a spray from the hose. Keep it wet by intermittent spraying for three days. The idea is to let it cure gradually and not crack.

Finally, use a pick to pull out the form boards, then fill in the trenches with soil. Drop some grass seed on it and the job is done. You've got a driveway that will last indefinitely.

OUTDOOR LIGHTING

For security and increased outdoor living, light is the key element.

There's no question but that outdoor lighting is given short shrift by most homeowners. It shouldn't be. Properly used, it can do many things, such as make the patio an enjoyable place to dine, accent plantings, extend time for outdoor games, add a measure of good looks to the house, and make the house safer—safer to walk around and safer against burglars.

A variety of bulbs and an even greater variety of fixtures are available to let you arrange outdoor lighting as you like it. First, the bulbs.

TYPES OF BULBS

Incandescent. These bulbs are usually just for illumination; they have no decorative aspect, such as casting colored light on a favorite planting. They are available from 10 to 150 watts. Ones over 25 watts need to be shielded from the elements by a fixture or they will break.

Projector (PAR) bulbs. These are spot and flood lights, used for both decoration and illumination. They are made of hard glass and won't break because of weather conditions. Both flood and spot types are available with clear glass lenses in 75 and 150-watt sizes. In addition, 100-watt floods are available with lenses in a variety of colors, including red, blue, green and yellow.

Vapor Projector Bulbs. These look like flood and spot lights but produce a blue-green-white light that flatters most foliage. An admedium socket and a ballast must be used with them. Weather-proof fixtures

With suitable lighting, the concept of outdoor living can be richly enjoyed at night.

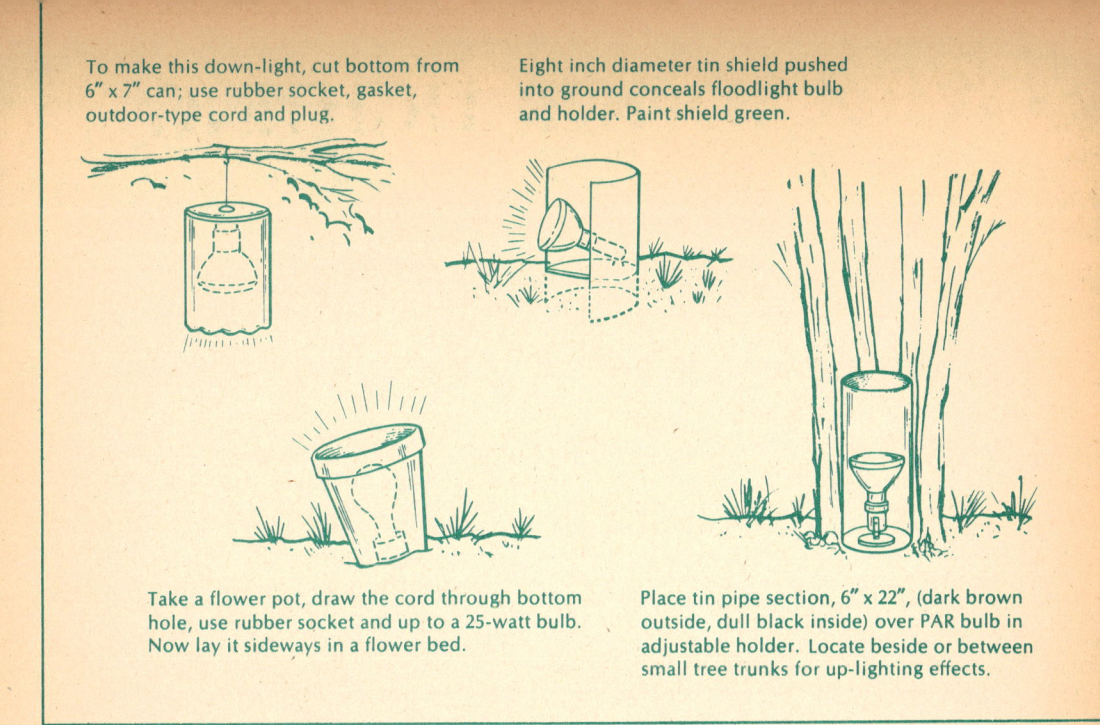

To make this down-light, cut bottom from 6" x 7" can; use rubber socket, gasket, outdoor-type cord and plug.

Eight inch diameter tin shield pushed into ground conceals floodlight bulb and holder. Paint shield green.

Take a flower pot, draw the cord through bottom hole, use rubber socket and up to a 25-watt bulb. Now lay it sideways in a flower bed.

Place tin pipe section, 6" x 22", (dark brown outside, dull black inside) over PAR bulb in adjustable holder. Locate beside or between small tree trunks for up-lighting effects.

A variety of offbeat but interesting outdoor light can be made by any handy homeowner.

complete with ballast, cord and plug are available.

Fluorescent Tubes. These throw out a horizontal line of light and are usually used for lighting fences or hedges. They must be housed in weather-proof fixtures (not exposed, as PAR bulbs may be). One and two-tube fixtures are available for permanent mounting or for use with ground spikes (discussed later). Fluorescents can be had from 4 to 40 watts.

Yellow Bulbs. Available in 60-, 100-, 150- and 200-watts. The color of these bulbs is less attractive to insects than ones that emit a plain, white light.

Decorative Bulbs. They come in clear, white or iridescent finishes, usually used in entrance fixtures with clear glass panels. Available in candle and flame-shapes from 10 to 60 watts.

Christmas Bulbs. While normally thought of as strictly a bulb for Yule time, may also be used in lanterns or strung, exposed, to create a festive effect.

TYPES OF LIGHTING

Fixtures for lighting can be broken down by end use: floodlighting (and spot lighting), step-path-border down-lighting, up-lighting and accent lighting.

Flood and spot lighting, whether the light is directed up or down, is usually done with projector (PAR) bulbs. There are stake types—you screw the bulb into the fixture socket—then drive the stake into a ground and swivel the bulb wherever you wish; types that can be fastened to the house; and ones that simply stand on a small base. As mentioned, projector bulbs come plain and in colors, making them good for illuminating as well as accenting the beauty of your home.

Step-path-border fixtures are designed to illuminate steps, paths, borders and the like for either safer walking or good looks. They're usually 8 to 30-inches tall with shades (tops) 6 to 18-inches in diameter. Shade designs range from graceful flower shapes to a straight, contemporary look. You can get these fixtures in portable models, or wired to be connected to a junction box and underground cable. The portable type comes with cord and plug and is driven into the ground.

117

When selecting a fixture for steps, paths or border, select ones that don't have bright glass or plastic parts that will cause glare, and can hamper vision. These fixtures usually utilize bulbs that range from 10 to 100-watts.

Down-light fixtures are designed to illuminate large areas such as patios, terraces, flower beds, driveways and lawns. Fixtures can be hung from tree branches or attached to tree trunks. They vary in shape from ones that look like a birdhouse to cones cylinders and lanterns.

Other down-light fixtures mount on the ground. They are either portable or wired so they can be connected to underground cable. They should be of a scale and design to spread light patterns over an area 20-feet or greater in diameter. For this they should be 30 to 65-inches high with shade diameters of 15 to 23-inches. The most popular ground-level type is the "mushroom" unit, which has a wide, flattish top. Other fixtures may resemble pagodas. Others have simple contemporary lines.

Up-lighting is accent lighting of trees, shrubbery, and fences and is most often accomplished by locating fixtures on the ground, pointing them upward. Hence, the term up-lighting.

Fixtures here are usually simply functional, not fancy. PAR and R (reflecting type) bulbs are most often used. To maintain an unbroken expanse of lawn it is often necessary to bury fixtures partially or completely below ground. Root conditions may dictate location, but generally they're located 3 to 5-feet from the tree trunk.

To produce a two-dimensional effect rather than a flat look, direct two up-lights at an angle on the object. To "wash" a wall or fence with light to front-light a long border or to silhouette foliage, try lines of light from fluorescent fixtures. The most popular size fluorescent fixtures accept 15-watt, 18-inch; 20-watt, 24-inch; and 48-inch, 40-watt tubes.

There are also a variety of fixtures for accent lighting that are ornaments in themselves. For example, you can get ones that are concealed in "rock," "toadstools," "driftwood" and other garden-like objects

Small down lights spiked into ground provide illumination and accent the colorful plantings.

← WEATHERPROOF OUTLETS AND BOX

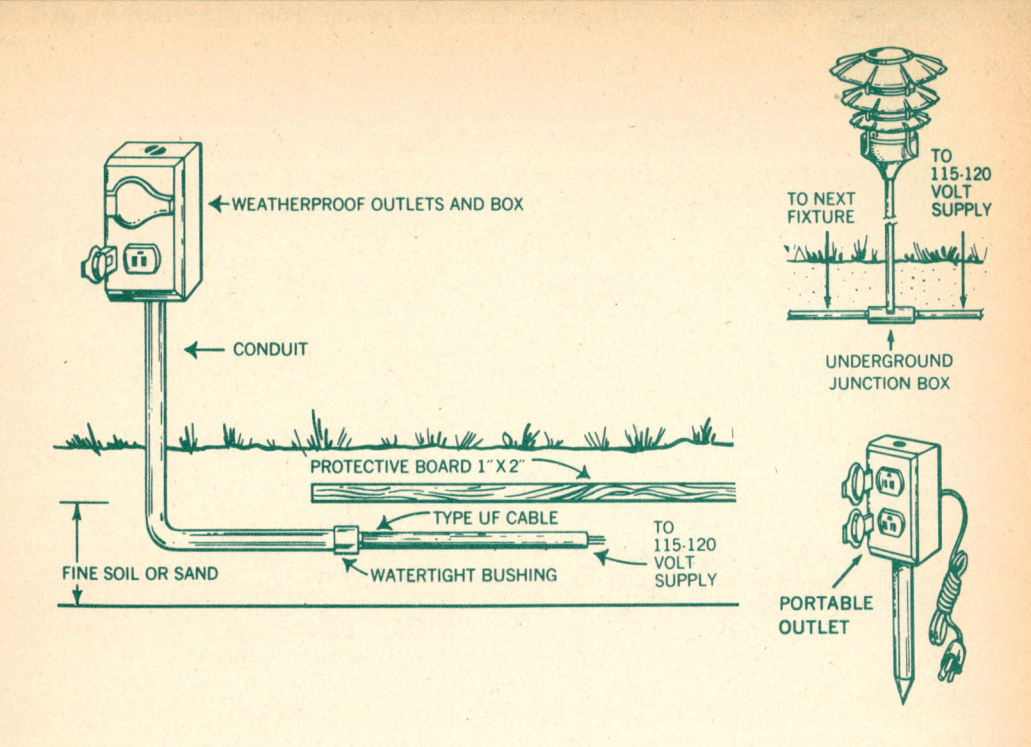

← CONDUIT

PROTECTIVE BOARD 1" X 2"

TYPE UF CABLE

TO 115-120 VOLT SUPPLY

WATERTIGHT BUSHING

FINE SOIL OR SAND

TO NEXT FIXTURE

TO 115-120 VOLT SUPPLY

UNDERGROUND JUNCTION BOX

PORTABLE OUTLET

Above, setting up outdoor outlets. Below, some of the many different styles of lights.

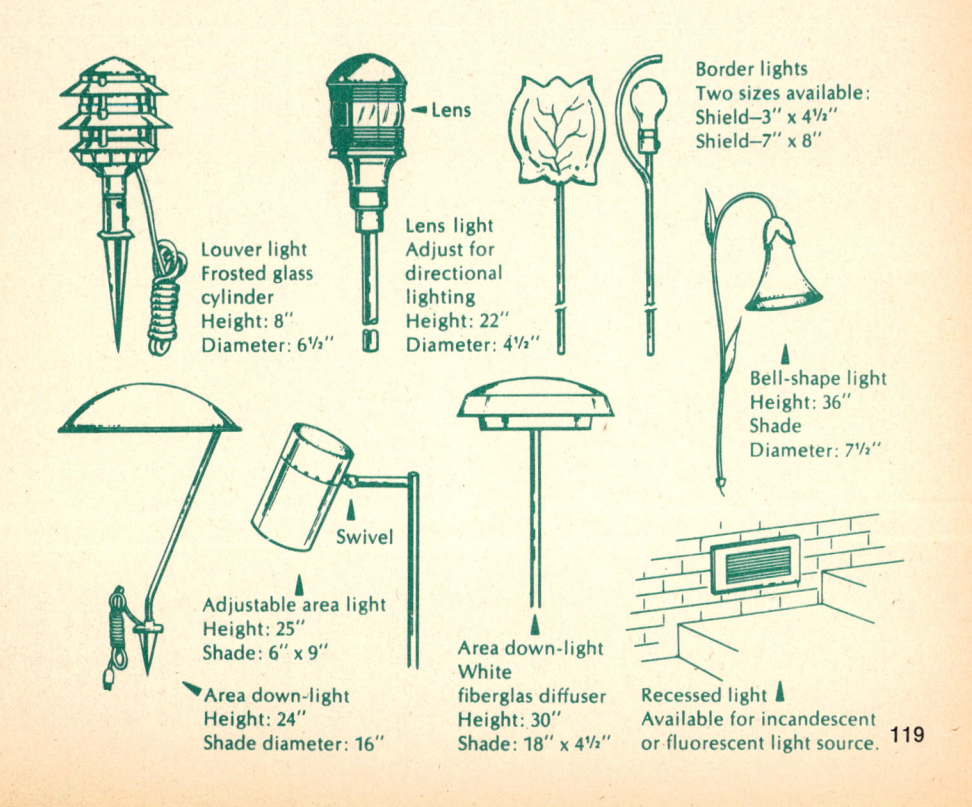

Louver light
Frosted glass cylinder
Height: 8"
Diameter: 6½"

← Lens

Lens light
Adjust for directional lighting
Height: 22"
Diameter: 4½"

Border lights
Two sizes available:
Shield—3" x 4½"
Shield—7" x 8"

Bell-shape light
Height: 36"
Shade Diameter: 7½"

Swivel

Adjustable area light
Height: 25"
Shade: 6" x 9"

Area down-light
Height: 24"
Shade diameter: 16"

Area down-light
White fiberglas diffuser
Height: 30"
Shade: 18" x 4½"

Recessed light ▲
Available for incandescent or fluorescent light source.

(including "lily pad" lights that can be used in water).

Entrance lights—the ones that go on one or both sides of the front door—are also available in various styles and should be picked to match house architecture. If possible, select types that are open at the bottom or covered with glass to give useful down-lighting. For softer, less glaring light, choose fixtures with frosted glass. If you use coach lights, you'll need supplementary lighting, since coach lights are mainly for decoration.

TEMPORARY WIRING

In setting up outside lights, you can make a temporary or permanent arrangement.

Temporary wiring utilizes outdoor type extension cords (use at least No. 16 wire) plugged into the nearest outlet in the garage, on the house or in the house. These cords come in lengths of 25-, 50- and 100-feet with sockets and plugs molded of weatherproof rubber. You'll also likely need at least one outdoor-type portable convenience outlet fixture, which is mounted on a stake that is pushed into the ground. Extension cords and outlet fixtures are available in two-conductor and three-conductor grounded types; get the latter kind.

To aid you in getting the light desired at the various points on your property, use garden fixtures with a built-in outlet. Since you will be using regular house current for setting up the lights, be sure not to overload circuits. Don't exceed 1600-watts on a 15 ampere circuit, or 2000-watts on a 20 amp one.

Your temporary lighting setup can last indefinitely. But it can also give you insight into what you want for a permanent arrangement. Make sure to locate cords so no one will trip on them.

PERMANENT WIRING

You can do permanent wiring if you're handy and know the electrical codes in your area. Otherwise, it's a job for a professional.

The job is done by first digging trenches for the wire you're running, each trench 18-inches or so deep. Basically, then, it's a matter of running ground burial (type UF) cable, which contains the wire, to weatherproof outdoor outlets or to underground junction boxes on which fixtures can be permanently installed. To effect your lighting scheme you can work in portable convenience outlets, fastening them to the house, fence, post, tree or other locations. Locate the equipment—permanent or portable—so it does not interfere with lawn mowing, garden work or traffic.

Key element in running circuit for outdoor lights is transformer. It is commonly available.

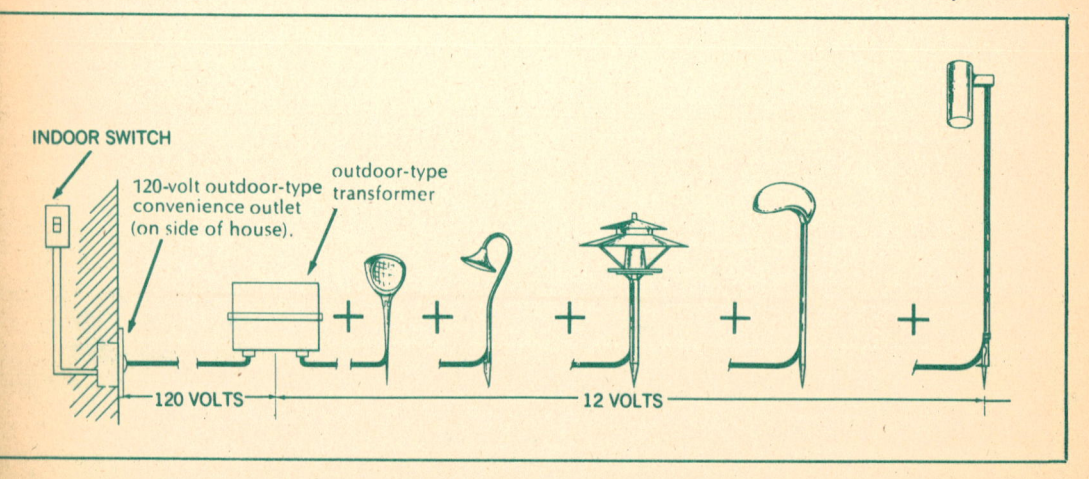

Provide separate circuits for outdoor lighting, with a switch controlling each, from the house. For best results in planning and for knowing locations for repairs —make a sketch of the wiring layout for ready reference. If you wish, you can also install an electric-eye or timer to control selected lighting units so your grounds will be lighted at dusk whether you're home or not.

LOW-VOLTAGE LIGHTING

We've been talking about light sources, fixtures and wiring designed to be used on standard household current of 115 to 120-volts. There is another system that is handy for outdoor lighting: the low-voltage type.

This system utilizes special bulbs, fixtures and wiring and operates on 12-volts, the same voltage used to run a toy train. The heart of low-voltage lighting is a voltage-reducing transformer which reduces the 115-120-volt supply down to 12-volts. Transformers are weatherproof and are easy to connect to an existing house outlet. Fixtures may then be easily connected to the self-sealing cable that sprouts from the transformer. Methods of doing this vary from manufacturer to manufacturer; see the specific instructions for how to do the job. You can get fixtures that are portable (they spear into a cable placed on the ground) or permanent where the fixtures are supplied with a conduit mount for attaching to a terminal box and underground cable.

Light level from low-voltage lighting is not powerful, but it can serve a variety of lighting purposes:
- Up-light small plants and trees
- Down-light steps, paths, foliage
- Dramatize pool or reflecting fountain
- Highlight statue, flower bed
- Accent-light wall, fence or patio
- Create shadow patterns.

Bulbs used for low-voltage systems differ in size and shape from 120-volt bulbs, and also are usually known by number rather than wattage. Usually, they range in "watts consumed," as between 7 and 35-watts. Also, they usually have a shorter life than the 120-volt types.

The low-voltage system has a number of advantages. First, it's easier to install than

When setting post, be sure to anchor it in a stiff mix of concrete. Premix is fine.

Well-located spotlights can be used to accent plantings, and provide home security.

the 120-volt type. If desired, you can relocate fixtures along the resealing cable with ease. Also, most 12-volt bulbs cost less to replace and operate and, not unimportantly, the 12-volt system is very safe. Even if you were to grip a bare wire you wouldn't get a bad shock.

Perhaps the best way to use the low-voltage system is in conjunction with the 120-volt one. Large, tall trees and big-area lighting needs can be handled by the 120-volt system, with the accent work done by the low-voltage one.

SAFE-WIRING HINTS

1. Only work when ground is dry.
2. Have one switch to control outdoor current; turn off all current while you're working.
3. Use only weatherproof equipment outdoors—cords, plugs, sockets, connections, fixtures, whatever.
4. Tape temporary connections with electrical tape, and elevate them to keep them out of puddles.
5. When a bulb comes with a rubber gasket, use it. It creates a seal around the neck of the bulb to keep water out of socket.
6. Let a professional wire underwater lights.

SETTING POSTS AND GARDEN LIGHTS

Wood or metal posts, particularly those that carry weight or are subject to lateral stress should be set solidly in concrete. Hole should be about 8-inches in diameter and a minimum of 24-inches deep with greater depth a requirement in deep frost areas. Do not use a form in the hole as concrete must have contact with soil for maximum strength. Coat below ground section of wood posts with creosote and metal posts with a rust inhibiting paint. Pour in about three quarts of water. Set post in hole and pour in dry concrete mix. Tamp material as you pour to mix the water with the concrete. Check occasionally to be certain post is vertical. Crown the top and smooth with trowel. Allow concrete to harden one week before putting strain on post.

LIGHTING TRICKS

• Accent lighting (from above and below) of trees, plants and other landscape features should be in addition to soft, sometimes tinted, direct or reflected lighting. Overall flood lighting such as used for protective lighting tends to "whitewash" a garden, creating a flat and monotonous appearance.

• Best results can be attained through the use of a number of fixtures, not just one or two. Fixtures are designed for different uses and to do different things. Know a fixture's versatility and how it distributes light.

• Light hazardous spots: steps, paths and walks. Avoid fixtures at these locations with bright and glaring glass or plastic portions. Conceal all bulbs to keep glaring light out of viewer's eyes. Also consider your neighbors' right to privacy. Select fixtures with shields or shades to hide the light bulb. Thick shrubbery, hedges, and so forth, can act as a shield for bulbs or utility fixtures. Rule: see the effect, not the bulbs.

• Use tinted light sparingly on white statuary, walls, trellises and fences; more vibrant colors in pools and fountains and for parties. Use white or blue-white light on flowers—nature has already colored them superbly.

• A little light goes a long way in the nighttime garden. Don't over-light. As a rule, the lighting results should be more subtle than obvious.

• Light is most effective on flowering plants that are white or light pastel in color, as they reflect more light. The same is true for trees with light-colored or shiny bark. Dark colors absorb light, and require more of it.

• Water reflects light like a mirror. Keep this in mind when locating units near water. Reflected lighting effects can be charming or annoying and glaring. Locate lights near water with care.

• Except for ornamental designs, fixtures should be inconspicuous. They are usually a mottled green to blend in with foliage.

• For greater dimension and effectiveness, light an object from more than one direction. This technique applies particularly to statuary.

BUDGET LANDSCAPING

It's possible to have your home beautifully landscaped on a budget.

Watering is one key to landscape beauty.

Landscaping Arrangements

Landscaping is something that can cost a lot of money if it's done on the basis of impulse buying or plantings and unplanned placement. On the other hand, it's something that can be done quite well and with a minimum outlay of cash if careful planning—a thorough analysis of the property—is done first. And you will end up with beauty around your home—a natural framework, if you will—that only planned landscaping can achieve.

MAKE A PLAN

Before you make any plant selections (and tips on these will be presented later), take out paper and pencil and draw a plan of your house. Draw, in scale, the house and plants around it full size; nursery book catalogs show these. Make an aerial view, showing all paths, walks, fencing, existing plants and trees, anything that is a permanent part of the property. Also make a front view of your home, and one of the back.

Armed with this, you'll know how to fill in the gaps. When selecting the plants and trees they should, of course, be good looking. But their color, texture and shape should harmonize with one another, much as the pieces of clothing of an outfit should go together well. And this holds even if the main purpose of the planting is not beauty, but something else. For example, a screen planting may be for privacy. But it should also tie in aesthetically.

While beauty is important, do pick plantings that are easy to maintain. You can get to dislike beautiful but fast growing shrubs that require hours and hours of trimming.

FRONT OF THE HOUSE

The front of the house is, of course, stage center when it comes to landscaping. There are no rigid rules to follow for landscaping it properly, but there are principles that have been known to work well.

If you have no trees on your lawn, and the lawn is not very large, planting one or two can form a focal center of attraction. For the purpose, you'll want to pick a tree that not only has lovely flowers or fruit,

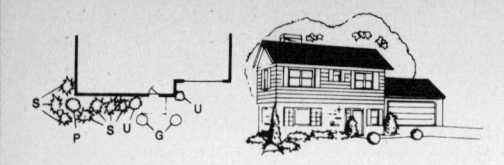

Salt box house could feature spreading juniper (S), upright juniper (U) quite well.

Combination of savin, upright juniper, yew, and boxwood work well for this house.

Only a few plants are used here—but quite effectively. The key is good placement.

Tall plants at corners (pyramidal arbivortae) complement shorter upright junipers here.

For low, flat house, spreading juniper (S), Upright juniper (U), Pyramidal Yew work well.

Upright yew (U), Globe Boxwood (G), spreading yew, pyramid yew go well here.

Upright juniper (U), Juniper Andora (S), and Pyramidal arborviat (P) dress up land here.

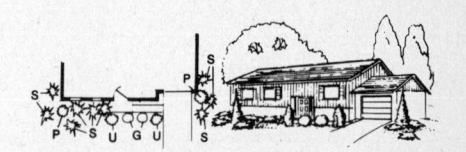

Juniper savin (S), upright yew (U), pyramidal yew (Y), globe boxwood would be fine here.

but good form, good-looking bark, foliage or buds. Good choices would be holly, Japanese red maple, weeping Japanese cherry, flowering crabapple, magnolia, white birch or dogwood (The author is partial to the latter, which he has on his own property).

Plant the trees where they can be seen from the street and the inside of the house.

To save the pesky task of mowing around them, plant some sort of ground cover around them—something such as pachysandra, creeping myrtle or ivy—and ring the cover with stones... looks good, too.

The rest of the lawn can remain as is. But you can also cut down on maintenance by planting additional ground cover plants, shrub borders and beds of

Planting a flanking walk makes a nice approach to this house. Use small plantings.

flowers that bloom annually (called annuals), such as petunias, that require hardly any care. You can also cut lawn maintenance down by having certain areas covered with gravel, or installing paths or colorful stone, brick or the like.

ALONG THE FOUNDATION WALL

The plantings that go next to the house form a framework for it and should be thought over carefully before installing. When landscaping errors are made, it's here. How often, for example, have you seen a glut of overgrown plants stacked against a foundation?

Landscaping needs here will vary, of course, but these tips should be helpful.

Flanking the front door is a good spot for an evergreen that will grow between 3 to 5-feet high. You have a good choice between needled and broad-leafed types. Among the former there are juniper, dwarf Alberta, spruce, yews, and some kinds of pine. Among the broad-leafed types, you have laurel, rhododendron, leucothoe, holly, boxwood, euonymus, andromeda, and azaleas.

Directly under windows, low plantings that are wider than they are tall work well. There is a great variety available. You can peruse these in nursery catalogs.

For the corners of the house, up to three shrubs—ones that grow to be less than house height—will serve well to soften its lines. Very good here are holly, upright juniper, pyramidal aborvitae, Japanese yew, spirea, hemlock, beauty bush and firethorn.

In general, evergreens are popular for foundation plantings because they stay green over the winter. But there are deciduous shrubs that can be used with evergreens to add color contrasts, such as everblooming hydrangea and Japanese quince, among others. You can also use vines, evergreen and deciduous, for contrast. If you want a vine to climb a masonry wall, consider evergreen Baltic ivy or wintercreeper. You can also get vines that flower . . . clematis, silver lace, and climbing hydrangea are three. These are suitable for walls, porch posts and trellises.

When putting foundation plantings in, it's a good idea to arrange them in a gentle curve, rather than a straight line for naturalness. Also, don't jam plants together. Place them so that some individual plants are emphasized and others are grouped together. When evaluating how plants will look in relation to one another, consider the size and shape, then the color and texture. If the plants you select will take a while before reaching full size, you can use ground cover to fill in the gaps.

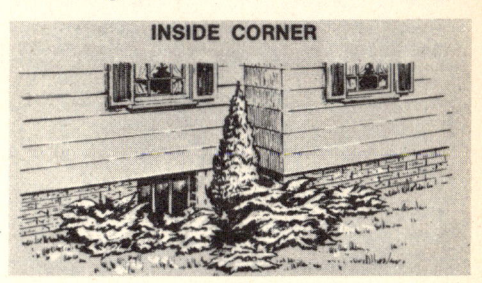

One way to handle inside corner of house.

Round off outside corners for good looks.

Here, the ultimate in natural shade, courtesy of ancient tree that "grows" from the patio.

Another option: plant annuals in the gaps until the plants grow up, then use them elsewhere.

AROUND THE PROPERTY

There are a variety of things you can do around the property. In front, if you want privacy, you can plant any of a number of tall, thick hedge plants such as arborvitae, Japanese yews, Cannart juniper, Persian lilac, Japanese holly, mock orange, Amur privet, alpine currant and hemlock. You could also use these for live fencing any other place on the property, or perhaps as a windbreak next to a patio.

If you just want a nice border—no privacy—for the property, you can use a short hedge. Among those good for this purpose are California privet, wintergreen, barberry, drawf winged euonymus and boxwood. Many of these don't require much upkeep; floribunda roses are a prime example.

If you have the room, you can also plant along the sides or rear boundary of the house to provide a sort of pretty boundary line. A line of taller flowering shrubs behind a line of shorter ones can work well here. For good looks—a non-hodgepodge appearance—use only one or two kinds of shrubs.

Plants may also be used to line driveways, paths and the like. If you use them for a driveway, make sure they're low if small children are in the area. You want to make sure that they'll be seen.

PATIO AREA

As mentioned above, you can enclose the patio area with hedges of varying kinds (the same kinds recommended for the front). This can provide privacy, as well as shelter from wind.

Plantings may also be used to isolate the eyesore of garbage cans, and the storage

Sprinkler head from Toro is well recessed in the ground, won't interfere with mowing.

unit if you wish. Another trick is to isolate the children's play area with low hedges. Remember to keep this area in view from the rear windows.

SHADE TREES

An important aspect of outdoor living is a good shade tree. You'll have to consider its size, the degree of shade it gives, whether it creates problems (some trees shed seed pods or fruit in abundance), its color in autumn. In general, you can get excellent value in large trees with American beech, sweet gum, red or green ash, black walnut, sycamore, honey locust and many of the maples, hickories and oaks. For a smaller tree, good value can be gotten from flowering dogwood (though it sheds petals profusely), yellowwood, golden raintree, Japanese pagoda.

One tree will usually be sufficient for the average yard. In larger yards more than one may be necessary. To check the shade pattern, hold a long pole as tall as the mature tree, in the spot you will put it and observe its shade pattern. Do this in the summer, for that's the time you'll want the shade, and the sun will be in the proper position.

To save some money on shade trees, you can get large flowering trees. A couple of these can be better, on a small lot, than one large non-flowering type.

FLOWERS

The greatest advantages of flowers, of course, are beauty and color. When using these marvels of nature, however, moderation is the key. Too many flowers can give your landscape a hot-house, gaudy effect that you'd be better off without. Rather, use the flowers to highlight all green or relatively subdued areas of plantings. You can use them at the foundation, against masses of shrubs, perhaps at a fence, or to soften the corners of walks or driveway. Using them as clumps or islands throughout the lawn is usually overdoing it.

It's best to combine only two or three different color flowers, either in contrasting or complementary colors. If you're using flowers in front of shrubs, let them build in height from front to rear, letting the shrubs serve as a dark background to the color. If you have a lot of area, use warm-color flowers in abundance since they tend to visually shorten it; cool color flowers will make a short area seem longer.

The most inexpensive flowers are the annuals. If you're a beginner, the flats of these sold in gardening stores every spring are the best bet. Perennials can be added later (These refer to plants that live more than two years).

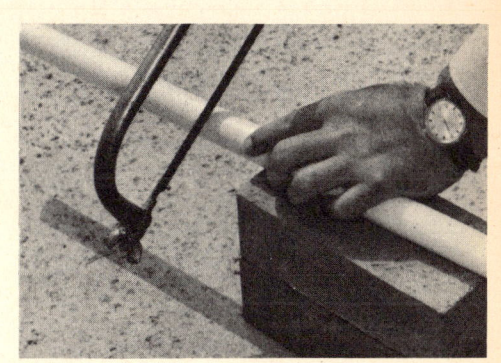

Plastic tubing cuts easily with an ordinary hacksaw. It is practically indestructible.

Good feature of plastic system is that parts screw together easily—no soldering needed.

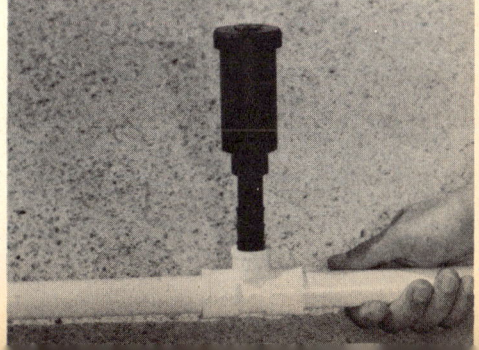

PLANTING

Always plant as soon as possible. If you can't get plants in the ground rapidly, unwrap them, moisten the roots and cover them temporarily with equal parts of peat moss and soil.

Also, prepare the ground well. For flowers, mix peat moss and a complete fertilizer into the ground before planting—seek the dealer's specific advice here. If you're planting a tree or shrub also seek advice. Tip: The hole should be twice the size of the root ball and the soil should be enriched as for flowers.

To help insure your success in the first place, stay away from fantastic bargain plants—you'll likely get stuck. Also, avoid the packaged plants sold in many non-nurseries—these are likely to be in poor shape because the dealer has kept them under poor conditions too long.

AN UNDERGROUND LAWN SPRINKLING SYSTEM

Most people want a healthy lawn because it's good-looking and adds value to the house. But a healthy lawn has other values. It helps control dust, holds soil runoff, keeps mud out of the house and can serve as a safe, comfortable play area for the kids.

One of the keys to a healthy lawn is regular watering. And it is here that an underground, automatic system, such as the Toro Moist O'Matic one shown here, can shine. It provides a simple, relatively inexpensive way to water without the usual hassle of having to remember to turn the hoses on on summer days, or lugging hoses, or running after a "walking" sprinkler. And, most important from the point of view of the health of the lawn, the system will provide the right amount of water—automatically—to the various areas, or zones of your lawn.

COMPONENTS

Components for the system are mostly plastic, making them easy to work with. Flexible tubing runs from a control box to a galvanized valve assembly screwed to an outside faucet. From each valve, other plastic pipe runs through narrow trenches made in the lawn (and, of course, covered with sod). At certain points there are either wave sprinklers or pop-up sprinklers connected to the pipe.

LAYING OUT THE SYSTEM

The only really tricky part of installing the system is deciding the amount and kind of equipment you need, and where to put it.

The easiest way to do this—and it's free—is to let your dealer do it. Just give him the details he needs. Make a sketch of your property in scale that shows plantings, flower beds, trees and permanent parts of the property. Also, what the gpm, or gallons per minute rate of your water supply is (you can get this from your water company). Keep a copy of the sketch so you'll know where not to rototill or plant in the future.

DIGGING THE TRENCHES

After securing the layout for your property, you lay out the PVC pipe in the finished position it will occupy. To install the pipe, use a flat spade to turn back the sod to a depth of 4-inches. Then place the pipe in the trenches, tamp in place with a board, pull sod back and tamp it down. At certain points, you'll need to attach sprinkler heads, and make other pipe connections with ells, T's and the like. The pipe is simple to cut with a hacksaw or sharp knife; hold parts together with stainless steel clamps.

The pipe must also be hooked into the outside faucet. For this there is a galvanized fitting on which you screw plastic regulator valves. These can be individually adjusted with a screwdriver.

Each of these valves is connected by flexible tubing to the control box. This has a simple wiring system—a common neutral and a hot wire from each head in each sprinkling zone to its respective valve and then to the box. The box is plugged into house current.

The box can control up to four sprinkling zones or stations. These can be four wave sprinklers (they oscillate back and forth) or pop-up sprinklers. Each station can be set to go on from 3 to 60 minutes. And it has the capacity to be turned on automatically every day, or every other day. The system allows a great deal of flexibility for different watering schedules.

INDEX

Index Key:

Chapter heads are in capital letters
Bold face numerals indicate a photo
Italicized numerals indicate diagram

A

ABC's OF BUILDING STEPS, 104-109
accessibility, **5**
A PLACE FOR YOUR CAR, 94, 103
asphalt, 8
all-weather carpeting, 23
aluminum nails, 39
anchored posts, 39

B

bankrun (sand), 111
BARBECUES YOU CAN BUILD, 50-57
barbecue
  brick, *51*
  gas, 51, **52**
  location, 50
  pit, 53, **54, 55**
  stone, 55, 56, 57
base cabinet, **77**
benches, *46*
benches, connected, *47, 48*
benches, three-deck, *47*
blocks, 17, 20
  how to make, 18
  installing, 20
  laying, *17*
  shape, *17, 18*
brick, shades, 6
  edging lawn, 59
  how to lay, *60*
  mailbox, **60,** *61*
  patterns, *17*
  on sand, *16, 19*
building a single step, 105
BUILDING PATIOS, 16-22
BUDGET LANDSCAPING, 123-128

C

carpentry, 69
carpeting, indoor-outdoor, 25
carport No. 1, 94, *96, 97, 98*
carport No. 2, 94, 97, *99, 100, 101*
carport No. 3, 94, 97, *102, 103*
  drainage, 95
  finishes, 97
  foundation, 95, 98
  rafters, 97
  roof, 95
  setting forms, 98
  storage units, *103*
cement-sand mixture, 18
ceramic tile, 77
cinder blocks, 56
Colotrym aluminum, 44
concrete, 7, **9,** 17, 21, 22, 27, **53,** 56, 61, **104,** 106, 107, 110
  finishing, 114
  pouring, 113
  removal, 110
  staining and dyeing, 27
construction, wet, 20
COOL WAY TO BEAT THE HEAT, 87-93
cross braces, 38
cross buck table, **49**

D

DECKS TO DELIGHT, 28-35
  construction, *29*
  hexagonal deck, 33, *34*
  multi-level, **30**
  parquet, *31*
  posts, 30
  raised, 33, **35**
  skirtboards, 31
digging trenches, 128
DOOR, INSTALLING IN PATIO, 10, 15
  construction, *11*
  door frames, *11*
  location, 13
  sliding glass, **10**
  styles, 10
DRESSING UP A DRAB SLAB, 23-27
DRIVEWAY, BUILD A NEW, 110-115
  board forms, 110
  build for strength, 111
  concrete, 110
  curving driveway, 115

E

edge for the lawn, 58
epoxy adhesive, 23, 27
evergreens, 125
excavations, **112**

F

fasteners, rust-proof, *47*
fences, 78-83
  basketweave, 82
  block, 79
  board, 81
  brick, 78
  chain-link, 79
  installing, 82
  picket, 82
  plastic, 79
  shrubbery, 79
  split rail, 82
  stockade, 82
  stone, 78
  wood, 79
FENCING FACTS, 78-86
fiberglass-reinforced plastic, **36**
fill (loose), 9
flagstone patterns, *19*
flooring, resilient, 23
flooring, seamless, 24
flowers, 127
form boards, 110, **112,** 115
foundation wall, 125
free-form concrete pool, 66
free-standing shed, 71, **72,** *73, 74*
frp patio covers, *37, 38*
FURNITURE, OUTDOOR, 43-49
  fold-away, 44, **45**

hinged, 43
redwood, 47

G

gables, double, *41*
gates, for fence, *84, 86*
grass, simulated, 25, **27**
gravel, *17*
greenery around patio, 124

L

LANDSCAPING ON A BUDGET, 123-128
    keep lawn healthy, 124
    plan patio and garden, 123
    setting lawn posts, 122
    start planting early, 126, 127, 128
ledger boards, *32*
LET (NOT) SUNSHINE IN, 36-42
logs as paving discs, *16*
LIGHTING, OUTDOORS, 116-122
    accenting the trees, 119
    border lights, 117
    down-light fixtures, *117,* **119**
    floods and spots, 117
    fluorescent tubes, 117
    incandescent, 116
    lighting tricks, 122
    low-voltage, 121
    projector (PAR) bulbs, 116
    safe wiring, 122
    tinted lighting, 122
    transformer, *120*
    vapor projector bulbs, 116

M

MISCELLANEOUS PROJECTS, 58-67
moldings, 38
molding strips, 38

N

nail holes, predrilled, 38
nails, aluminum, 39
neoprene, 39

O

outdoor buffet, **77**
outlining the patio, 20

P

painting, 26, 27
panels, corrugated, **40**
patio chair, 44
patio, dry, 20
pools, 87-92
    above ground, **88,** 89
    cost, 87, 88, 89, 92
    excavation, 92
    filter, **90,** 92
    heaters, 91
    in ground, 87, 88
    plywood, **92**
    vinyl-lined, 88, 91
posts, 41-102
    barbecue, **53**
    bracing, 82
    brick mailbox, 61
    carport, 102

fences, **81,** 83, 85
    metal-based, 41, 42
plan your plants, 123
planting at corners, 125
plywood cabinet, **70,** 71
plywood, rough sawn, 72
plywood, sheathing, 69, 71
PRIMER ON PATIOS, 5-9
privacy, 6, 78

R

rafters (shed), 69, 71
retaining wall, **58,** 62, 64
retaining wall, dry, 62
retaining wall, wet, 64

S

sand, 16, 17, 19
sandbox, 65
sanding block, 43
sawhorse, chain saw, 66, 67
sheathing, 69, 71
shed door, **75,** 76
shed, double doors, 72, 76
shed, lean-to, 68, 69
slab, cracked, 26
sprinkler components, 128
sprinkler system, 128
stair railings, *109*
steps, 104-109
    building forms, 106
    concrete, 106
    dimensions, 104
    fill materials, 107
    finishing, 107, 109
    footings, 106
    non-slip finishes, 107
    simple wood, 106
stone border, *21*
stone curbing, 58
stone edging, 58, 59
storage, hanging cabinet, **68,** *70,* 71
STORAGE, OUTDOORS, 68-77
stringers, *108*
stringers, anchoring, 108
sun screens, 36

T

table trays, 44
tile, usages, 7
treads and risers, 108
trees, shade, 127
tubing, plastic, 127

V

ventilating, 37

W

watering, 123
wiring, permanent, 120
wiring, temporary, 120
whirligig, backyard, *65*
wood block paving, 22
wood covers, 40
wood rounds, 8
wood stairways, 108